Praise

Sparking Le

"You cannot effectively advocate and teach psychological safety unless you truly live it. Upon meeting Barbara Singer, you immediately feel comfortable. She does not just do this simply as a friendly gesture. Her warmth is genuine yet also effective at creating the conditions where clients, employees or whomever is involved to bring their best selves and ideas forward. The foundational skills that make her so adept at executive coaching are the same that make Barbara a successful businesswoman."

— Lori Costew,
Former Chief Diversity Officer
Ford Motor Company

"I have had the opportunity to see Barb Singer be open and vulnerable in very sensitive situations. As a non-diverse woman seeking understanding and wanting to lead with compassion in the aftermath of George Floyd's murder, Barb set aside her preconceptions about societal norms and joined a focus group comprised mostly of ethnically diverse women working through a complex web of fraught emotions. Her openness to learning and having her most deep-seated beliefs challenged created a space that allowed the rest of us to share our true thoughts and feelings, our pain, fears and scars that had been ripped open in that time. Watching her understanding evolve and learning to recognize the subtle (and sometimes not so subtle) iniquities that have always existed in her surroundings gave me a slight sense of hope in those very dark and heavy days. Barb is not simply learned in the area of psychological safety, it is a way of life for her that shows up in all that she does, professionally, socially, personally. Participating in the focus group wasn't enough for her, she wanted to share her learnings with her Executive MBA classes at Notre Dame. On two occasions, we were invited to share our perspectives on diversity with her classes, bringing first-person, lived experience and expertise to the curriculum. Barb Singer, personally and professionally, is a living testament to the powerful impact of creating spaces that provide belonging and psychological safety."

— **Carmen Ortiz-McGhee,**
Chief Operating Officer
National Association of Investment Companies

"When I think of a person, a leader that has the ability to create psychological safety bubbles, three words come to mind: Ethical, Empathetic, and Empowering. During the 16 years that I've known Barb Singer, I have watched her use these three traits to create places of psychological safety which allows others to offer their insights and viewpoints, even if they are counter to everyone else in the room. It's quite amazing to witness, and it's one of the reasons she's been one of my trusted advisors and confidantes for years."

— **Michael Desiderio,**
Executive Director
Executive MBA Council representing
over 220 top global business schools

"Barbara Singer and Executive Core have been assisting in the development of Michigan's healthcare leaders for more than a decade. Physician's, Allied Practice Providers, and non-clinical leaders have all benefited from Ms. Singer's facilitation of the long-standing MHA Healthcare Leadership Academy (HCLA) in partnership with major state universities. Her contribution of one-on-one coaching is what set this program apart from any other. To date, when asked what an alumnus of the MHA HCLA remembers most and made the difference in their career, consistently praise for Barbara's contribution is always front and foremost."

— **Gary Roth, DO,**
Chief Medical Officer
Michigan Health & Hospital Association

"Barb Singer has been an invaluable mentor to me, our MHA team, and hospital leaders from throughout our membership. Her authentic approach is incredibly welcoming–and watching her in action at numerous leadership programs and events over the years, I have learned from her first-hand how effective creating psychologically safe bubbles can be."

— **Brian Peters,**
Chief Executive Officer
Michigan Health & Hospital Association

Sparking
LEADERSHIP

*Cultivating Psychological Safety to
Retain Top Talent, Boost Employee
Engagement, and Ignite Innovation*

BARBARA SPENCER SINGER

JONES MEDIA
PUBLISHING

Sparking Leadership: *Cultivating Psychological Safety to Retain Top Talent, Boost Employee Engagement, and Ignite Innovation*

Author, Barbara S. Singer, MA, MCEC

Jones Media Publishing
10645 N. Tatum Blvd. Ste. 200-166
Phoenix, AZ 85028
www.JonesMediaPublishing.com

Disclaimer:

The author strives to be as accurate and complete as possible in the creation of this book, notwithstanding the fact that the author does not warrant or represent at any time that the contents within are accurate due to the rapidly changing nature of the Internet.

Printed in the United States of America

12 11 10 09 08 07 06 05 04 03 02 01

ISBN: 978-1-948382-80-9 paperback

To my children, Sophie, JK, Spencer, Oliver,
and Emze who challenge me every day to test
my assumptions and expand my own understanding
of psychological safety. And for Bob who helps me
weather the storms of life with love and grace.

Table of Contents

Safety in Belonging

We walk into spaces
each and every day
where we wonder to ourselves,

Do I belong here?
Am I valuable?
How does my story change the narrative?

All answers found in the unseen
these threads that run from you to me
our humanity making us all one in the same

we go beyond our expertise
each moment our knowledge evolves to wisdom
we are reminded of who we are

through each and every share
our tears create the overflow
a river of connectivity

the beautiful, sacred bond of psychological safety and security.

— Korie Griggs, 2023

Introduction

A friend and colleague who had been leading talent management globally at a consumer goods company called me up and confessed that they had invested millions in teaching employees about psychological safety but didn't measure how much they had or if the global training had improved employees' sense of psychological safety. He called me from Australia to chastise me. He reminded me that my firm had been measuring psychological safety for 14 years. And my prior firm, now owned by Korn Ferry, had also been measuring two decades before that. He said it was time to get busy and start letting people know about our work. So here I am.

Sometimes the most obvious things are right in front of us. After years of studying top leaders, I discovered a simple way to measure a person's ability to grow psychological safety—my purpose in writing this book is to demystify how a leader grows a zone of psychological safety that fosters financial results, lowers regrettable loss of talent, and encourages innovation. I am writing this book for corporate leaders, government officials, and those passionate about community impact. It starts with the bubble of psychological safety our leaders create for their stakeholders and teams.

In another international consumer company with 100 years of success (likely a household name for most of us), we were able to study the CEO's top 30 high potentials. What we discovered was profound. 1) From our measures, only 5 of the 30 were truly high potential, 2) Of these 5, their teams were achieving extraordinary financial results in some of the world's toughest markets, leading initiatives that were innovative and often had not been tried before, had the highest employee engagement scores, and the lowest regrettable loss of talent. What was their secret? People reported these leaders grew strong psychological safety bubbles they fostered upward, laterally, and with direct reports.[1] Since then, we have been able to see this pattern company after company. We also saw the pattern foster inclusion of more diversity in graduate business education. We saw this pattern forward anti-hate initiatives being led by leaders in communities. Strong psychological safety bubbles are helping our health systems recover after the pandemic.[2]

Working with an attorney reporting to the mayor of one of the most violent cities in America, he is using the concepts in this book to teach black communities how to more safely navigate police pull-overs. Since the murder of George Floyd, tensions have escalated between police and black citizens during routine pull-overs. Even if the person was in the act of committing a crime, we wanted to increase a feeling of safety among both police and the citizens. It begins with the statement by the driver, "I want you safe. I want me safe. How do we go about doing that?"

---

[1] Executive Core, "How We Measure and Grow Psychological Safety in Our Client Organizations."

[2] Singer, Sara J., Shoutzu Lin, Alyson Falwell, David M. Gaba, and Laurence C. Baker. "Relationship of Safety Climate and Safety Performance in Hospitals." *Health Services Research* 44, no. 2p1 (March 12, 2009): 399–421. https://doi.org/10.1111/j.1475-6773.2008.00918.x.

I knew I had to get busy writing this book when it occurred to me that something so simple can keep our police officers and citizens safer.

I trust you will embark on a personal exploration of yourself while you read this. We can all work to develop better psychologically safe bubbles in a time when people feel their workplaces are more toxic than ever before. I also hope you will hold your teams accountable for maintaining bubbles of psychological safety alongside accountability for results. Ultimately, I hope you will lead from a strong psychological safety bubble wherever you go. When my bubble is strong, I am operating at my best. And when my bubble shrinks, I feel it in my heart, and it challenges my sense of hope.

You can be a master at creating bubbles of psychological safety without a strong conviction about the direction of change you want. If so, you aren't leading. . . yet. Someone recently asked me why I used the term bubble instead of space. I replied, "you can take a bubble with you wherever you go. It expands up, sideways, and downward. It can be large or small. It surrounds you." For others, the metaphor of holding an umbrella of psychological safety over others works better. Bubbles and umbrellas travel with you wherever you go. I also affectionately use the acronym, DTT: designed to travel when we write performance summaries for executives. A bubble is DTT. There are people who grow magnificent bubbles of psychological safety for others yet fail to lead or influence.

While studying and teaching influence for more than 25 years, I appreciate that leadership and influence go hand-in-hand. I have been honored to watch and learn vicariously from a diverse array of successful leaders. I have coached, facilitated, and navigated my own, often tumultuous life, with influence concepts by my side. My colleagues constantly challenge and teach me new ways to think about our ability to open people's minds and hearts. One thing that I fiercely believe is that you, reading this now, are far more influential than you realize. You have leadership characteristics inside of you that are dormant and underutilized. You have creative ideas that are just ready to formulate.

Your influence skills don't just apply to your loved ones, your work situation, or your immediate team. If you project an exceptional bubble of psychological safety and grow your repertoire of influence languages, you can accelerate your impact everywhere. The days you make the biggest difference are often the days you feel most downtrodden. The things you end up influencing others may surprise you.

Influence without integrity can so easily become evil. I believe that fiercely. Inspirational figures in history began with a well-developed moral compass and deep self-awareness. They did not simply make time to be reflective, they took the time to understand how other people experienced them in both feelings and cogent thinking. They fought against fear and urged people to find creative solutions that achieved positive outcomes both for people and project output. When you are truly influential, you are willing to be well educated on multi-perspectives, engaged in multi-scenario thinking, and willing to test your own assumptions to see if they are faulty or limited in some ways.

During the decade I taught at Notre Dame, our classes considered the acts of Ray Anderson, the deceased CEO of Interface Carpet Tiles. When customers began asking Ray what he was doing for the environment in the early 80's, he didn't have much of an answer. So he began educating himself on the environment and industry. At the time, carpet manufacturing was a leading polluter. Ray counted his company among them. He called it a spear to the chest when he realized that his company was hurting the environment for generations to come. He set out on a path to educate, learn, relearn and inspire leaders around the world to rethink how business could be both profitable and environmentally responsible. Interface remains a model for how companies can become environmentally sustainable.[3]

When you are influential, you are a bridge builder—not a brainwasher. I have had the unique opportunity as a consultant to have ring side seats to CEO scandals, watched people who were whistle blowers take tremendous hits to their careers, and seen scores of people hurt by leaders' poor decision-making. In nearly every situation, these leaders made decisions in isolation, quieted voices who disagreed with their approaches, and failed to build bridges across their enterprises with people who might have challenged their priorities, values, and logical evaluation criteria. In the fall of 2001 and the winter of 2002, I was leading a global engagement to help the regional leaders of sales for WorldCom formulate their strategies to grow market share. I was impressed with their hard work and creativity. Some of the leaders in emerging markets like Africa were among the most innovative. I was confident that their plans would work. When it came time to present the global plans, we could not get a meeting with anyone from senior leadership. It was highly unusual that a company of WorldCom's size would invest in such a global sales undertaking without presenting their plans at the top of the house. The senior leaders seemed distracted from activities that would fill their pipeline in the year to come. Cynthia Cooper was the brave whistleblower from the audit department who discovered $3.8 Billion in overstated balance sheet numbers.

---

[3] Adam R. Luqmani, Matthew Leach, and Da Jesson, "Factors behind Sustainable Business Innovation: The Case of a Global Carpet Manufacturing Company," *Environmental Innovation and Societal Transitions* 24 (September 1, 2017): 94–105, https://doi.org/10.1016/j.eist.2016.10.007.

Eventually, the number grew to $11 Billion. An already financially troubled WorldCom filed for bankruptcy, CEO Bernie Ebbers was sentenced to 25 years in prison, and Cooper who was asked to stand down multiple times, stayed until WorldCom emerged from bankruptcy and became MCI. She never re-entered corporate employment again.[4] She became a consultant and wrote a book. I have met at least a dozen "Cynthia Coopers" over the course of my career. Years after the experience, most whistleblowers suffer from shaken trust caused when working without a psychologically safe bubble. Their confidence is often impacted as they remember how many times senior leaders questioned their integrity. For many, they opt out of a traditional career or have trouble finding a job.

Fear, suspicion, and control are the enemies of ethical influence.

Our world needs you to activate your ability to influence with integrity. But before you can be fully influential, leaders can master the ability to build bubbles of psychological safety. You then spark leadership in others. The environment we create for people closest to us will be remembered longer than the projects we complete or the initiatives we launch.

Our world needs psychological safety. And we need you to be more influential at home, at work, in your neighborhood, online, and in writings electronically. Our world needs you (and me) to also try to be resilient and compassionate with ourselves when we fail. A colleague recently reminded me how important it is to show ourselves grace. It made me think of National Geographic's Rogue Trip with Bob Woodruff and his son Mack.[5] As a combat journalist who nearly died in 2006 in Iraq when a bomb exploded

---

[4] Cynthia Cooper, *Extraordinary Circumstances: The Journey of a Corporate Whistleblower*, 2008, http://digilib.umpalopo.ac.id:8080/jspui/bitstream/123456789/407/1/0470124296__Extraordinary%20Circumstances%20The%20Journey%20of%20a%20Corporate%20Whistleblower.pdf.
[5] On Disney+. "Rogue Trip," n.d. https://ondisneyplus.disney.com/show/rogue-trip.

causing massive skull damage to him; he re-learned to walk, talk, and write again with his children's help. Years later, he and his son Mack travel back to the parts of the world where he served as war correspondent for ABC and now reports on what is good in those parts of the world. He finds people who turned in their guns and are finding new ways to support their families and support their communities. He now reports on the good in the world and second chances.

Stop reading right now and look at the last text you sent, the last social media post you sent, the last email you composed, the last video you made, the last conversation you had hoping that something at work would change for the better.

This is your benchmark. I challenge you to make the next communication even more powerful, inclusive, welcoming, inspiring, fact-based, playful, and clear. The juxtaposition of this kind of communication seems almost contradictory. Yet, when done well, it is very balanced.

This book is both a collection of stories and a practical guide for:

- Psychological Safety: Promote an environment of psychological safety wherever you go
- Performance Mindsets: Promote your mindset two levels higher
- Impact: Live your career like you are not afraid of getting fired
- Balanced Communicator: Be both a great listener and someone who can be assertive
- Languages of Influence: Speak all the languages of influence fluently
- Coaching & Coalition Building: True influence sparks leadership in others

- If first you don't succeed, try something different: Dialing into the other's person's radio channel
- Predictors of Success: increase your odds of success
- Strategic Conversations

Chapter 1

Psychological Safety Bubble

"We learned that there are five key dynamics that set successful teams apart from other teams at Google. . . . Psychological safety was far and away the most important."

— Julia Rozovsky,
People Analytics Manager at Google[6]

I recently had a perfect day. By most accounts, it was an
ordinary day. You might even argue that perfect doesn't exist.
Perhaps. But the feeling and glow of that day was pervasive and
lasting. I woke up next to my husband who greeted me with a
smile and a kiss, we rounded up the children at home that day
and went to a religious service, our youngest spoke with deep
appreciation about his camp experiences, I greeted new and old
friends afterwards, went to brunch with a friend, laughed and
talked, did chores at home, visited with a neighbor, answered
some email, finished a work project with ease, and had dinner
together as a family. Sounds like an ordinary day, but in my mind

---

[6] "Five Fifty: Is It Safe? – Desktop," n.d. https://ceros.mckinsey.com/is-it-safe-
desktop/p/1.

it was extraordinary. I was loved, safe, encouraged, productive, spiritual, and amused by my family's antics. My house was not clean, I could see dust and dog fur, there were weeds in parts of my garden, leaves needed to be blown, my email was chiming at a fast clip, I had three documents to prepare for clients, and the car needed to be washed. I did not care. The day was perfect. I have a sort of positive hangover from reflecting on all that was good that particular day. Imagine your perfect day. What thoughts and feelings are you having? Imagine your perfect day at work, home, volunteering or traveling. For most of us, ideal days share common characteristics. You are safe, respected, challenged, productive, playful and have made a difference. You are likely surrounded by interesting people who are kind, respectful, and helpful. If you are lucky, you have many loved ones that contribute to the perfect day. I was solidly in the bubble. I have more days in the bubble than outside of the bubble. And as I've aged, I've gotten better at growing that bubble for others. At work and in our communities, psychological safety bubbles are game changers.

Leaders Who Create Bubbles of Psychological Safety

- Define it
- Communicate it
- Know what it takes to grow it
- Measure it
- Coach it
- Spark leadership in others

I encourage leaders who create bubbles of psychological safety to take a moment to enjoy life in the bubble. If there is any downfall to this topic, it's that people tend to spend more time talking about what psychological safety isn't rather than seeing where it exists. And perhaps many of us spend more time talking about leaders who fail to create a bubble of psychological safety than acknowledging those that do. Make a list of all the people in your life that have made you feel safe, appreciated, respected, and encouraged. How did they create an environment where you could be productive and creative?

Executive Core professionals have been researching psychological safety in the workplace for over twenty years. We have correlated leaders that create environments of high psychological safety with better financial performance, lower regrettable loss, more innovative success.[7] High levels of psychological safety promote workforce engagement, job satisfaction, and organizational advocacy. We also expect to report higher levels of patient outcomes when hospitals achieve high organizational levels of psychological safety. The inverse is also true. According to a 2022 MIT Survey, 30 million US workers think their workplace is toxic. Toxic workplace people are 10.4 x more likely to quit, report burnout, and report mental health challenges.[8]

In this chapter we explore how to easily define psychological safety for others, identify competencies that grow psychological safety among teams, have you think about your own leadership, and learn ways to communicate what psychological safety is to their workforce to foster increased performance.

---

[7] Singer, Barbara. "Preventing Executives at Risk of Derailment." *Lore International White Paper Series.*, 1993.

[8] Sull, Donald, Charles Sull, and Ben Zweig. "Toxic Culture Is Driving the Great Resignation." *MITSloan Management Review*, January 11, 2022. https://sloanreview.mit.edu/article/toxic-culture-is-driving-the-great-resignation/.

Made popular by Harvard's Amy Edmondson, Ph.D.[9]— psychological safety at its core helps people feel:

- included,
- safe to learn,
- safe to contribute, and
- safe to challenge the status quo.

> "Psychological Safety is a belief that the context is safe for interpersonal risk-taking–that speaking up with ideas, questions, concerns, or mistakes will be welcomed and valued even when I'm wrong. It's a sense of permission for candor."
>
> —Amy Edmondson

Psychological safety occurs when people can perform at the top of their capacity by sharing their ideas, concerns, mistakes, and hopes for the future.

- People enter work with a belief that they will not be embarrassed, humiliated, or isolated by sharing
- As leaders, we promote or detract from a psychologically safe climate
- Psychological safety is the most important factor to workforce engagement and performance

When present, people can perform at the top of their capacity by sharing their ideas, concerns, mistakes, and hopes for the future.

---

[9] Edmondson, A. (1999). Psychological Safety and Learning Behavior in Work Teams. Administrative Science Quarterly, 44(2), 350-383. https://doi.org/10.2307/2666999

As leaders, we promote or detract from a psychologically safe climate. A psychologically safe bubble is manufactured when a leader employs a subset of skills we study using the 360° assessment Psychological Safety and the Languages of Influence™[10]:

- Adheres to high ethics
- Is authentic
- Is willing to discuss tough issues
- Refrains from intellectual bullying
- Accurately portrays information
- Uses power associated with his/her position appropriately
- Creates an enjoyable atmosphere
- Is sensitive to other feelings

The resilient leader maintains those skills even under stress. The bubble then inspires people to not only do their best but to manufacture positive bubbles of their own. For many, this bubble becomes positively contagious. For others, they detract from the bubble by not demonstrating the skills above. Leaders can establish bigger psychological safety bubbles by holding themselves and their stakeholders accountable for how they conduct themselves. We measure psychological safety using a 6-point Likert scale in 360° degree feedback. We have identified thresholds. The highest level of developing a bubble of psychological safety we highlight in green. Moderate levels yellow. And levels that

---

[10] Executive Core, and Barbara Singer. *Psychological Safety and the Languages of Influence*. 360-assessment. 2.0. Executive Core, 2023. https://executivecore.com.

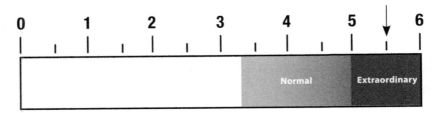

Rating Scale:
6 = Exceptional
5 = Very Skilled
4 = Good
3 = Competent
2 = Slightly Unskilled
1 = Poor
0 = Not Used or Observed

are damaging relationships with frequency—the red zone. We hope this book will help you consistently lead from the Green Zone. Using a 6-point scale, most leaders are in the yellow zone and score between 3.2 and 5.

Something amazing happens when leaders are maintaining a bubble of psychological safety for their stakeholders at the 5.5 level. We see strong correlations of happy, highly engaged team members, innovation, financial results, and low regrettable loss. It is not unusual to see those people on rapid succession plans. Numerous studies of leadership have proven time and time again that the number one reason people leave an organization is that they have a toxic relationship with their supervising leader.[11] Quiet quitting is a bi-product too often of an employee perceiving

[11] Global Talent Trends: Data-Driven Insights Into the Changing World of Work. "Global Talent Trends: Data-Driven Insights into the Changing World of Work," n.d. https://business.linkedin.com/talent-solutions/global-talent-trends/archival/global-talent-trends-october-2022.

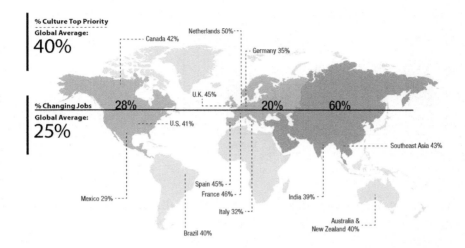

that they are not welcome to share their ideas or acknowledged for their efforts.

It's no secret that Employees Continue to Switch Jobs[12]...

And Seek a Stronger Culture

In 2022, we saw a peak in people changing jobs due to lack of positive culture.

70% of workers have experienced at least one form of harassment and abuse in their workplace last year A recent study by McKinsey shows the impact of high toxicity in the workplace and the advantages of low toxicity in the workplace.[13]

---

[12] LinkedIn and LinkedIn Talent Solutions. "2022 Global Talent Trends." The Great Reshuffle, 2022. https://business.linkedin.com/content/dam/me/business/en-us/talent-solutions-lodestone/body/pdf/global_talent_trends_2022.pdf.

[13] McKinsey Health Institute. "Moving the Needle on Burnout: What Does the Data Say?" McKinsey & Company, 2022. https://www.mckinsey.com/mhi/our-insights/moving-the-needle-on-burnout.

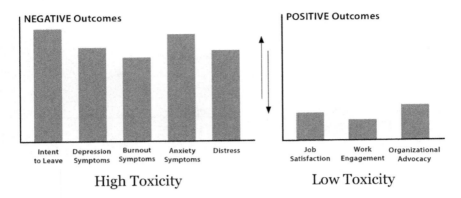

High Toxicity   Low Toxicity

We apply psychological safety to battle healthcare burnout. While giving a presentation to hospital leaders in 2023 (still weary from the pandemic and onslaught of financial pressures that occurred as a result of nurse shortages, higher priced traveling nurses needed, and higher cost of labor and goods in general), I pulsed an audience of 128 hospital CEO's, CNO's, CMO's and other medical leaders.[14] Here's what they shared about observable symptoms of exhaustion and cynicism in their respective organizations:

[14] Singer, Barbara and Iowa Hospital Association. "The Promise of Psychological Safety for Better Workforce Engagement And Performance." Workforce Engagement. *Https://My.Ihaonline.Org/Events/Calendar-of-Events.* Des Moines, United States of America, n.d. https://my.ihaonline.org.

Think about what symptoms of exhaustion and cynicism are apparent across your organization.[15]

Estimate Your Workforce %. Is your workforce generally more cynical or purpose-driven? To what degree are they exhausted or energized? Plot where you think employees land.

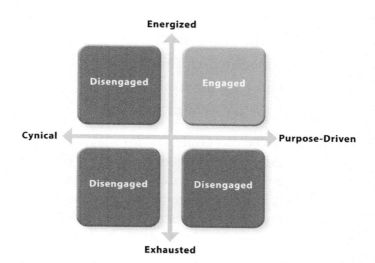

It occurred to us first anecdotally and then became clear when we studied the statistics for levels of significance, that truly superior leaders at companies are already promoting a culture of learning on the job, every day, everywhere, at every level. In our landmark study in 2016 it was clear that these leaders came from different regions and different functions. And finally, even among your top 26, leaders who achieve both business results and promote a learning culture are likely rare.[16]

So what was their secret?

[15] Melikian, Ana. "The PIE Method." Blubrry Podcasting, September 1, 2023. Accessed October 10, 2023. https://anamelikian.com/the_pie_method/.
[16] Executive Core, "How We Measure and Grow Psychological Safety in Our Client Organizations."

They were much higher than average and exceptionally rated (average 5.5 score from a 6 point measure) for the following:

- Adheres to high ethics
- Is authentic
- Is willing to discuss tough issues
- Refrains from intellectual bullying
- Accurately portrays information
- Uses power associated with his/her position appropriately
- Creates an enjoyable atmosphere
- Is sensitive to other feelings

This list continues to be our guidepost for making psychological safety accessible and simple for leaders to build. We continue to demonstrate that psychological safety is closely tied to financial performance, employee engagement, customer retention, and employee retention using our scales in the Psychological Safety & the Languages of Influence™. Our measures align with Amy Edmondson's work as few others do. We've also tied psychological safety to student satisfaction and team learning— and we've applied psychological safety to instructional design to radically increase access to higher education to black, brown, female, students in the Midwest—we continue to influence over 225 universities around the world to do this on a global scale.

> *As someone who has the privilege to lead EMBAC, an organization that represents business schools which offer masters degrees for the executive and working professional populations, I've seen first-hand how the academy is striving to be a difference maker in the development of leaders. Through robust education, they are helping leaders see the real advantages of placing a very high value on diversity of thought, on creating a space where employees feel safe to discuss the hard issues using soft skills. Embracing the idea*

that it's the right thing to do is important and understanding it creates a real business advantage is critical.

The very fact that executive coaching has made its way into Executive MBA programs, speaks to the academy's willingness to go beyond education and provide practical insights for leaders on a very personal level.

I've had a front seat for over 16 years, watching how schools of business themselves are working hard to find ways to incorporate elements of diversity, equity, and inclusion into their own organizations. It's not that they "have arrived" but they realize creating healthy work environments can be a competitive advantage in attracting high quality talent to careers in education administration, which can't compete on salary with the business world.

Michael Desiderio, Executive Director of the
Executive MBA Council

Sometimes knowing the opposite of psychological safety, helps us define it. I am grateful for the tough lessons and environments I worked in during my early career. Psychological safety was often low and I was an "only." Only female, only person under 40, only non-engineer, only American. . . And it also created some emotional triggers for me later in life that I had to manage. By the time I was in my late-30's, my personal life reflected significant holes in psychological safety as well.

One leader I had the honor of working with had come out of an abusive relationship with her father. As she became an adult she was passionate that she would create light hearted and kind environments for her co-workers. At home, she had a partner who supported her and provided an envelope of psychological safety. Her confidence grew along with her skill—and sense of humor. She worked very hard to develop psychological safety for her high-pressure client engagement team. While I worked with her, she was promoted and acknowledged by the senior leaders for her grace under fire with upset clients. The company did outsourced research for their large publicly traded clients, and this leader's team was exceptionally skilled at repairing relationships and getting projects back on track after set-backs occurred. While creating a bubble of psychological safety for her team in an otherwise volatile and potentially hostile client environment, this leader helped her team problem-solve project issues quickly. She helped save many strategic accounts as a result. Much of her wisdom came from a history of understanding what psychological safety wasn't.

With many teams, I have had them complete a simple exercise. You could do this with a team you lead or suggest as a member of a team that your team try this. List your organization's values. I did this recently with one state's largest community college system. It looked liked this:

The Values We Want	We sometimes do the opposite for our TEAM	We sometimes do the opposite for our STUDENTS	We sometimes do the opposite for our OTHER PARTNERS	We sometimes do the opposite for our COMMUNITY	We sometimes do the opposite for the ENVIRONMENT
EMPATHY We stand with our students, partners, and communities.					
ACCOUNTABILITY We deliver on our commitments.					
AGILITY We innovate, iterate, and transform.					
CONNECTIVITY We connect with partners to strengthen communities and ensure student success for all.					
We practice honesty, courtesy, and civility, respecting all. We believe in a college community inspired by collegiality, collaboration, and open communication.					

Identify times when your teams do the opposite of your organization's Values.

Think of ways your teams can help get the organization back on track.

When the leadership team began listing all the ways that faculty and staff behaved the opposite of their values, it was clear that each of those actions were hurting psychological safety.

When leaders understand what psychological safety is, how to define it, what it isn't, and how to start looking for signs it exists; they can better lead others. Create a roadmap like this one for helping an individual, team, or organizations.

EXECUTIVE CORE'S PSYCHOLOGICAL SAFETY ROADMAP

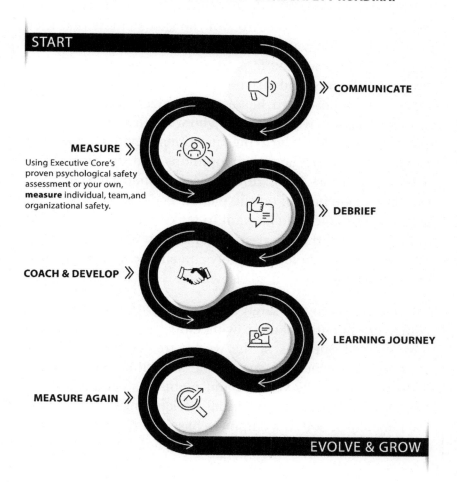

START

» COMMUNICATE

MEASURE »

Using Executive Core's proven psychological safety assessment or your own, **measure** individual, team, and organizational safety.

» DEBRIEF

COACH & DEVELOP »

» LEARNING JOURNEY

MEASURE AGAIN »

EVOLVE & GROW

Finally, without deep empathy, psychological safety bubbles shrink. Allow yourself to be a leader who can take on the perspective of others and feel deeply.

At the Ford Motor Company

Building psychological safety at an individual level can be simple but requires consistency and building habits. Ford Motor Company is a global, very complex and matrixed organization known for leaders proud of their 'stripes.' I regularly reminded executives of the vast shadow that they cast on the organization, and the need to make people feel included if they wanted to get the right input necessary for solving problems and driving the business forward. Like many companies, Ford has a strong meeting culture. The strongest leaders were the ones who welcomed people, made eye contact, asked clarifying questions, invited input and most importantly, gave their opinions and decisions after listening to others. Belonging is a basic human need common to every single person on the planet. People vote with their feet. Talented individuals want to make a difference at their organization; if their current organization does not provide physical and psychological safety and ensure they feel valued and respected, they will go elsewhere.

Building psychological safety at the organization level requires being very intentional at growing empathy. Our experiences have created our lens of the world; this is essentially 'the glasses' from which we see people and situations through. Although Ford sells vehicles and mobility solutions around the world to customers from all backgrounds, in the U.S., the majority of both the employee base and the C-Suite is the demographic of white male. Understandably, most would not know what life was really like for a woman or person of color, nor the experience of being "an only" in the room. As the Chief Diversity, Equity & Inclusion Officer, I created the concept of 'Listening Sessions', where the C-Suite leader met with a homogenous group of employees (e.g., women, African Americans, women of color, LGTBQ+, Hispanic/Latino, Asian Indian, Veterans, Caregivers, etc.). The leader was "an only" in the room and told explicitly to listen, not solve and only ask clarifying questions. The discussion points were simple but profound; what is it like to be me working at Ford Motor Company. The impact was significant for most; one leader said it was the most impactful hour of his professional life. I personally learned so much as I was the leader in the Listening Session with white males. It is not possible to design products, services and experiences that appeal to a broad audience if the needs are not listened to and understood. And if employees don't feel safe enough to share, at best the nuggets of wisdom are lost, but more likely a competitor will figure it out. While the sessions were designed for the respective leader's development, we had other positive outcomes. The meeting facilitator took anonymous notes in order to share recommendations for both policy/benefit changes with the proper business owners, and the participants felt more empowered to share perspectives more broadly with their teams. When you feel like you belong and have value, most often you can achieve things you previously did not think possible. When you trust who you are working with or for, optimism and ideas flow. Instead of wasting valuable energy working around a toxic person or system, productivity increases dramatically because all energy is on solving the problem or innovating.

Lori Costew, former Chief Diversity Officer
at the Ford Motor Company

Chapter 2

Communicating Psychological Safety

"Safety is the most basic task of all. Without a sense of safety, no growth can take place. Without safety, all energy goes to defense."

— Torey L. Hayden

Working with the head of communication for one of the world's largest pharmaceutical firms, I observed one leader setting the standard for communicating psychological safety. Their executive leadership team were disciplined communicators: decide, inform, ask. This helped when a new Chief Communication Officer inherited a group of individual contributors that had much to learn about teamwork. In a series of offsites, she set ground rules for operating with excellence in a bubble of psychological safety. Previously, they had felt in competition with each other, rarely getting recognition from their previous leader for teamwork. After working hard to coach and develop the team to avoid complaining about each other, she and outside coaching helped them replace that habit with mutual encouragement. They progressed rapidly.

The executive leadership team and CEO noticed. They could speak with one voice and pivot quickly. They received feedback that the team was consistently positive and uplifting when working with other teams. When the communication team had to navigate a series of natural disasters and a shooting, they communicated quickly and with compassion. One leader's emphasis on teamwork, psychological safety, and empathy did more to build the team in six months than a decade under another leader who hadn't. The Chief Communication Officer had also held very senior finance roles and operated well at the board level. She didn't hold back teaching her team what she knew and preparing them to navigate well at the most senior levels or when communicating with analysts. When she left the organization for another opportunity I know she was proud of the legacy she left, had several direct reports well prepared and ready to take her role, and knew the team would thrive on their own.

When we sabotage our communication, there are four common reasons:

- Imposter Syndrome[17]
- Dunning-Kruger Effect[18]
- Triggered (by Fear detailed in the SCARF Model)[19] or Fear of Loss of

---

[17] Clance, Pauline R, and Suzanne A. Imes. "The Impostor Phenomenon in High Achieving Women: Dynamics and Therapeutic Intervention." Psychotherapy: Theory, Research & Practice 15, no. 3 (n.d.): 241–47. https://doi.org/10.1037/h0086006.

[18] I want to give my 15 year old son recognition for reminding me to write about the Dunning-Kruger Effect. Kruger, Justin, and David Dunning. "Unskilled and Unaware of It: How Difficulties in Recognizing One's Own Incompetence Lead to Inflated Self-Assessments." Journal of Personality and Social Psychology 77, no. 6 (January 1, 1999): 1121–34. https://doi.org/10.1037/0022-3514.77.6.1121. Dunning, David (27 October 2014). "We Are All Confident Idiots". Pacific Standard. The Social Justice Foundation. Retrieved 28 October 2014.

[19] David Rock, "SCARF: A Brain-based Model for Collaborating with and Influencing Others," NeuroLeadership Journal, vol. 1, no. 1, December 2008, 44

- ○ Status . . . losing our importance to others
- ○ Certainty . . . not being able to predict the future
- ○ Autonomy . . . losing our sense of control over events
- ○ Relatedness . . . not feeling psychologically safe with others
- ○ Fairness . . . being taken advantage of or getting shorted
- ● Quietly quitting

Imposter syndrome is when we underestimate our competence and see ourselves as less competent than others who work with us.

The Dunning-Kruger Effect is when we overestimate our competence and think we are more informed than we actually are.

Triggered by fear occurs when we flee or fight because something that happens reminds us of a deep seated worry or fear from another time when we might not have been psychologically safe.

Quiet quitting happens when you don't actually quit your job but you do the minimum, stop speaking up in meetings, and otherwise check-out mentally. It's as if you work by the defeatist mantra, "why bother? No one is going to listen anyway."

I have had the honor of teaching alongside Lisa Lahey who authored the book (in partnership with Bob Kegan), Immunity to Change[20]. There is also a Harvard business article Lisa Lahey helped write that explains the concept briefly. Basically, we do the opposite of our goals (like communicating strategic ideas) because we have a deep seated worry that keeps us frozen. It is generally something we don't want to admit to others so it keeps us stuck. One finance leader shared his insight about his

---

[20] Kegan, R., & Lahey, L. L. (2009). Immunity to change. Harvard Business Review Press. https://hbr.org/2001/11/the-real-reason-people-wont-change

immunity to change. "I learned that the reason I have been so resistant to change in the past is because my subconscious self is trying to protect me from what it sees as dangerous. I have been resistant to changing my bad habit of saying "yes" to everything asked of me. It came out of a fear that others won't like me if I tell them I don't have the capacity to fulfill their request. After testing the waters and finding out that I am not in danger, I have been able to say "no" more!"

When are you at risk of sabotaging your communication? Why? At what cost to yourself, your team, or your organization?

At one of the world's biggest telecommunication firms we were able to study the top 500 leaders below the CEO by comparing results from a 360° feedback assessment[21], their employee engagement scores, financial performance, and performance reviews. These leaders had also been categorized as TOP PERFORMERS (ready now for promotion), FULL (solid performers not ready for promotion), or NOT YET FULL PERFORMERS (who needed performance improvement). We performed cluster analysis on the data and compared it against each leader's succession management rating. We discovered there were clear high potentials who viewed themselves positively as others did (well above a standard deviation above the norm). Then, there were solid performers not ready for promotion. They rated themselves a standard deviation lower typically than their stakeholders. (Imposter syndrome in action). And there was a clear correlation with people who were categorized as not yet full performers. This group rated themselves one standard deviation higher than their stakeholders (Dunning-Kruger effect in action). Stakeholders included direct reports, peers, senior leaders and others outside of the organization with whom the

---

[21] Singer, Barbara. Preventing Executives at Risk of Derailment. Lore International White Paper Series. 2019.

leader worked closely. As we coached solid performers it became clear that their imposter syndrome was holding them back from leadership opportunities.

Self Versus Others Comparisons by Performance Rating

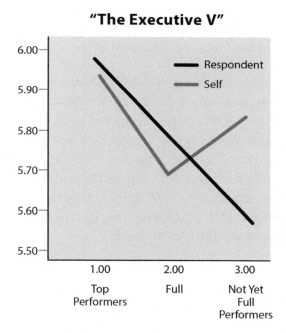

"The Executive V"

In our client work, I made simultaneous observations of the three rating patterns of High Potential Leaders, Dunning-Kruger Effect Leaders, and Imposter Syndrome Leaders the Executive V. We have also referred to the phenomena as the Awareness Index and it began to inform the next 20 years of my study of predictors of executive success. Where do you think you fall on the Executive V?

Communicating psychological safety requires showing sensitivity to your own experiences and the experiences of others. Most of us are triggered by a time(s) when we didn't feel safe. When you meet someone who has difficulty trusting others, chances are they have been a victim of violence, aggression, or some other form of depravity. Chances are you, the reader, has experienced moderate to extreme situations where you weren't psychologically safe or even physically safe. Talking about past situations where people did not feel safe is very likely to trigger symptoms of post-traumatic stress. You may be feeling some now. And yet, the path to psychological safety requires vulnerability.

Over 10 years while teaching at Notre Dame in South Bend, Indiana, it became a tradition in the first class of the Executive MBA to share a story that deeply impacted each individual as a leader. After establishing very strong guidelines for what safety means in a classroom, among a team, or in an organization; people should begin feeling safer to be authentic about who they are and their experiences. I have to tell you that these stories and the accepting, empathetic, and loving reaction of class after class of students restored my faith in humanity.

We are often taught to tell an elevator pitch about the highlights of our career and personal accomplishments. We are not always taught ways to tell the rest of the story. My life is certainly an example of that. While my resume and executive bio touts accomplishments, prestigious clients served, awards, publication, etc.; few realize I have become the mother to five children along the way. I suffered the tragic loss of my first husband after making partner in my firm in my late 30's after just giving birth to twin boys. I perhaps married too quickly following Scott's death and found myself in a marriage that was not psychologically or physically safe. My personal leadership benefited as I found the strength to leave, reinvent my life again, and continue raising my children as a single mother. It was an emotionally charged period of my life and an expensive lesson, and yet I stayed on my professional trajectory. At Notre Dame, during these storytelling sessions I always mustered the courage to go first. I was honest with my students about how my loving parents, spiritual beliefs, and hundreds of friends and family helped me rebuild my life and regain my confidence. I was brave enough to tell my own "beyond the resume" story. I could also comically tell the story of how, after just under a decade of being single, my 90+ mother subtly encouraged me to get back in touch with my childhood best friend who had recently been divorced. Today, I am happily married to my childhood best friend, and we enjoy a wonderful life together and fulfilling careers.

It was not unusual during "beyond the resume" introductions for students to share times in their life when they were not safe or someone they loved was not safe.

As I have come to know so many men and women who grew up in underserved and violent neighborhoods, a common theme emerges. One or perhaps a few special people in a young person's life saw something special in the person and nurtured it. Even in neighborhoods filled with violence, special people can still create bubbles of psychological safety that rocket amazing people to greatness. And those people in turn create bubbles of psychological safety for others. I can recall a story told by Corey Mays, former linebacker for the New England Patriots and former linebacker at Notre Dame about returning to the South Side of Chicago to go to church with family when he saw a gunshot victim. Corey picked him up, placed him in his car, and drove him to the ER. Corey also shared what it was like living in Chicago growing up while attending Morgan Park High School. Violence and death among the young men of the community was common. Corey's focus and mentors led him to be awarded a very rarely given full scholarship to Notre Dame for a public league athlete. After his NFL career had ended and he was earning his

Executive MBA, Corey carried team spirit, optimism, sense of fun, and comradery into the room every time I saw him. And he never failed to acknowledge the people who had believed in him as a child and young adult. These special individuals extended a psychologically safe bubble for him despite the violent neighborhood environment—in turn they sparked tremendous leadership in Corey.

In some cases, I have met people who share stories of losing their loved ones to violence. I had many students who were former military who earned their Executive MBA. For some, they had experienced trauma in combat. I had several students tell stories of what it was like to lead in combat during the 2004 second battle of Fallujah. When someone suffers from post-traumatic stress, they may get lost in the story and lose touch with people in the room and their reactions. They begin to re-experience images and feelings from times when their life and safety were endangered. Their sense of time is lost temporarily, and they begin to focus on details from the past. For those who care for them, we experience the storytelling as extremely detailed, and the person cannot seem to stop telling it. For some of us, their story becomes almost like a movie and we, in turn, become immersed in its telling. To bring the person back to the present requires an environment of psychological safety, love, acceptance, and deep empathy. And I might hazard a leap that spiritual (not religious which can be divisive but holistic spirituality) insight also helps. When a person has been triggered and is detached from the present, one of the most practical ways to bring oneself back is to focus on the details of what you see in a room and begin to describe them to yourself. The person who has been triggered will often be embarrassed and feeling vulnerable. When they begin to see faces of acceptance and empathy, it facilitates the person's return to equilibrium. Acknowledge their experiences and offer tremendous acceptance and support. They will need that to be authentically repeated over time. For some, PTSD recovery is a lifetime of work.

Before communicating psychological safety in our current society, consider the statistics. I was attending a Big Brothers Big Sisters public presentation in Indianapolis (Big Brothers Big Sisters of Central Indiana), led by Eric Saunders who is a leader there at the time of writing this book. Eric is also a poet and a storyteller. Indianapolis at the time of writing this is one of the most violent cities in America. Eric asked the audience of community members to raise their hand if they had attended the funeral of youth who had died violently. Nearly everyone in the audience raised their hand. He continued to ask until people had experienced five funerals of youth who died at the hands of violence. As a white woman who grew up in an upper middle-class family, my heart broke when the majority of the audience kept their hands up.

Almost half of all women and men in the US have experienced psychological aggression by an intimate partner in their lifetime. Women ages 18 to 24 and 25 to 34 generally experience the highest rates of intimate partner violence. Children witnessed violence in nearly 1 in 4 households. 30% to 60% of intimate partner violence perpetrators also abuse children in the household. 1 in 4 women (24.3%) and 1 in 7 men (13.8%) aged 18 and older in the US have been the victim of severe physical violence by an intimate partner in their lifetime. Workplace violence is also common and the leading cause of job-related deaths at work. Over 2 million Americans experience workplace violence a year and the numbers are growing.[22] One female military veteran

---

[22] Black, Michele C., Kathleen C. Basile, Matthew J. Breiding, Sharon G. Smith, Mikel L. Walters, Melissa T. Merrick, Jieru Chen, and Mark Stevens. "National Intimate Partner and Sexual Violence Survey." *2010 Summary Report*, January 1, 2011. http://hdl.handle.net/20.500.11990/250.

I met recounted her story of rape while serving. At the time, she felt pressured not to disclose the perpetrator who was powerful in rank and influence. She carried the emotional scars of the experience that colored her more positive memories of service. She no longer felt the military protected their own. The dissonance in her experience caused her to be silent for many years. When she finally shared her story in a work situation with high levels of psychological safety and mutual sharing, the men in the room became supporters, advocates, and spoke often about psychological safety. I count them among some of the most inspiring manbassadors I have met. Should any of you be reading this, you know who you are. And the woman remains one of the most remarkable leaders today I have also met.

I was speaking recently with a licensed therapist, Catherine Guerrero, who had been introduced to my approach of growing bubbles of psychological safety. She asked me if she could use our cards, our process, and our assessment in her work. I was intrigued. She mentioned that our cards made psychological safety more accessible to people. It could help them understand what a psychologically safe bubble entailed, and she could use this in her therapy to help a person grow stronger relationships by growing bigger bubbles of psychological safety. Or, depending on the person's wellness challenges, set boundaries and avoid people who were toxic and acting opposite to the cards. Catherine had also been called in to help after violent acts or incidents of workplace violence. She thought the 360° degree Psychological Safety and Languages of Influence™ would be a useful workplace measure after counseling traumatic experiences at work. After an appropriate time had passed, she thought she could use the assessment in work environments to see if psychological safety had been restored. There is much to be explored here, and Catherine challenged me to think of bigger applications for the tool.

A big part of psychological safety is to lead by example and be vulnerable and authentic yourself.

It starts with you and usually a good look in the mirror. Before you can communicate what psychological safety is for others, you need to understand how well they experience you developing a psychological safety bubble for them. None of us are perfect. My children will tell you that their feelings of psychological safety have been questioned in year's past when I am housecleaning. I am more likely to raise my voice and show my frustration after finding yet another sock and partially full candy wrapper lodged in the sofa cushions. Anytime you lose your sense of humor, you are at risk of losing your ability to keep a psychological safety bubble for others. That doesn't mean there aren't consequences. But if you've become emotionally hijacked and continually think about how awful the situation is then chances are you aren't in the green bubble.

If you'd like some feedback about how people perceive your leadership, consider completing the Psychological Safety Languages of Influence™ 360° assessment[23]. Before you communicate what psychological safety is, it is advantageous to first understand how well others see you developing a bubble of psychological safety for them. And you don't have to be perfect. Some of the best examples of leadership are when I've seen a senior leader apologize for interpersonal interactions that were likely perceived as intimidating, avoiding, threatening, insensitive, or not fully transparent. Even if being perceived that way was not their intent, if others experienced it that way, it is worth an apology. And a discussion to see how people communicate even more effectively in the future. Not all people

[23] Executive Core, and Barbara Singer. *Psychological Safety and the Languages of Influence*. 360° assessment. 2.0. Executive Core, 2023. https://executivecore.com.

want communication the same way. And we all make faulty assumptions about another person's intentions. Understand where you stand in your own psychological safety leadership bubble and be able to communicate exactly what psychological safety is to others. The leaders who do this consistently spark leadership in others.

A special level of attention to and care for the language we use is necessary when communicating about psychological safety. Growing up I remember so many phrases that were designed to elicit laughter in middle and high school and often ended up hurting the recipient. In a recent article written by Ella Washington for the Harvard Business Review, she summarizes some of the most common microaggressions[24]. I've heard each and it makes my heart heavy for the times I didn't speak up.

- "I didn't realize you were _____ — you don't look _____," signaling that a person of a certain heritage has a stereotypical look.

- "I believe the most qualified person should get the job," signaling that someone is being given an unfair advantage because of their race or gender.

- They _____(describe a negative trait or collective behavior. They bring it on themselves). Indicating that there is a pervasive trait among a certain community when you are not of that community.

- "You speak English so well — where are you really from?" signaling that people with English as a second language are generally less capable of speaking English. Or assuming that they are immigrants.

---

[24] Washington, Ella. "Recognizing and Responding to Microaggressions at Work." *Diversity and Inclusion*, May 10, 2022.

- "We don't have gender differences here anymore. Women have equal rights. Why do they have to be so emotional?"

- "It must be the hormones talking today."

- I'm not prejudiced but . . .

- "You don't seem like you grew up poor. You seem so normal and accomplished."

- "Wow, how did you get into that school? Did you play sports? Were you on scholarship?"

- "You are crazy and that's insane." "You just worry too much. You are going to die young unless you _____." "I get depressed too and this is how I get out of my funk. You should just _____."

- "I am so OCD about house cleaning" "I think he's a little autistic." "That's retarded."

- "So are you married? What does your wife do? (assuming that the person is heterosexual)"

- "She's not ready (for a promotion). She's got her hands full with kids."

- "You can work late. You don't have kids."

In other words, be careful with your words. The more plainly you speak, the more you question your own assumptions, and the more you seek to understand; the better you will be able to educate others about what psychological safety is. To help you in this journey, we want this to be accessible, translatable, and easy so we developed a set of cards that helps leaders explain what psychological safety is and how well leaders build their own bubbles of psychological safety. If you are interested in using these cards and their easy facilitation guide, visit executivecore.com.

And if you need to acknowledge someone else's microaggression, and are looking for appropriate ways to respond, I was impressed by the University of Illinois Urbana-Champaign (Grainger College of Engineering/Women in Engineering) guide to responding to microaggressions.[25] There is power in owning your own process of challenging assumptions and illuminating personal blind spots. "I noticed that you (your own specific observation of what they said or looked like). In the past, I didn't realize how statements like this might make someone feel. I doubt that was your intent. I learned _____."

Psychological safety is also important in the metaverse which is a term you may hear described in a variety of ways. I like to keep it simple. When you and the people around you have avatars interacting with other avatars online for a variety of purposes, (it started with my children's fascination of co-building Minecraft worlds with other people), psychological safety can be defined, communicated, measured, and sustained. It can also be shattered. A friend of mine who had just started dating again after 27 years of being married, was inexperienced about the dangers of the metaverse. As he began interacting with someone who espoused to be an attractive woman who needed help to escape an abusive relationship, he liquidated $15,000 of retirement funds to help her. When he realized that he had been phished, he was relieved to learn an FBI agent was reaching out to help him retrieve the funds. $40,000 later, with one elaborate scheme after another, he realized a group of people was impersonating the FBI and working together to deceive him. He was so embarrassed that he kept this crime a secret from his friends and family for months. Because the metaverse is an immersive emotional experience,

[25]"A Guide to Responding to Microaggressions – Women in Engineering," n.d. https://wie.engineering.illinois.edu/a-guide-to-responding-to-microaggressions.

any kind of verbal attack, deceit, or microaggression has more impact than in a traditional online setting. Staying in and promoting a psychological safe bubble in the metaverse requires thoughtfulness. Protecting your private information so others cannot mimic you is equally important. While I am encouraged that my children have all read (and watched the movie version) of Ernest Cline's 2011 novel, Ready Player One[26], people need a code of conduct for metaverse interactions. We talk about kindness and exuding the same code of conduct virtually as you would in the presence of your mother. Check out the metaverse-standards organization who provides a code of conduct on the topic.[27] I was impressed by the breadth of prestigious (metaverse operating) organizations represented on their board. Here is an excerpt from their code of conduct on promoting psychological safety in the metaverse.

Examples of behavior that contributes to creating a positive environment include, but not limited to:

- Using welcoming and inclusive language
- Being respectful of differing viewpoints and experiences
- Accepting and respecting constructive criticism from the community
- Showing empathy towards other community members

I thank them for this work and commitment to the topic.

---

[26] Cline, Ernest. *Ready Player One*, 2011. https://bibliotheques.vyvs.fr/recherche/ viewnotice/id/35815/clef/READYPLAYERONE-SPIELBERGS-WARNERHOM-EVIDEO-2018-4/retour_avis/14.
[27] Metaverse Standards Forum. "Code of Conduct — Metaverse Standards Forum," April 17, 2023. https://metaverse-standards.org/diversity-and-inclusion/ code-of-conduct.

PSYCHOLOGICAL SAFETY CARDS

Start with yourself. Ask yourself which two would be your

- Consistently top rated? If you completed our 360° assessment on psychological safety, would people score you in the "green zone?" for these top two?
- Bottom rated on your worst day? How might you fall in the yellow or red zone on days that are full of stress and anxiety?

We encourage leaders to communicate what psychologically safety is clearly and briefly. Use the definition from Chapter 1, psychological safety occurs when people can perform at the top of their capacity by sharing their ideas, concerns, mistakes, and hopes for the future.

- People enter work with a belief that they will not be embarrassed, humiliated, or isolated by sharing
- As leaders, we promote or detract from a psychologically safe climate
- Psychological safety is the most important factor to workforce engagement and performance
- Psychological safety is the main building block of culture

Here's a formula you can use:

- *Give each person the card deck.* Available at executive_core.com.
- *Ask them to read the first card's definition of psychological safety.*
- *Think of a time when they were working with a leader that created a deep level of psychological safety for them.*
- *Think of a time when they did not have an environment of psychological safety at work.*
- *Using the second card in the deck, ask each person to prepare to rate their leadership and how well they exemplify each element of psychological safety typically. . . and consider how this differs on a very high stress and frustrating day.*
- *Being solidly in the green zone or bubble is the goal.*
- *Have your group work in pairs or groups of three.*
- *Encourage discussion.*

- *Apply your discussion to future teamwork.*
- *Use the cards to quickly recap and revisit your group's level of psychological safety.*
- *Add the elements of psychological safety to your performance review discussions.*
- *Use the deck to acknowledge and recognize people who develop affirming bubbles of psychological safety.*

After you have a team event to introduce the concept of psychological safety, have people discuss their own accountability to grow an umbrella of psychological safety. Challenge them to commit to at least 3 things that raise the team's bubble of psychological safety both within their ranks, with more senior leaders, direct reports, and other peers. Ask them to give specific examples of what they will do differently. Finally, take action to follow-up on their commitments, provide feedback, and encourage them to keep it up. When you see team members sparking leadership in others, celebrate them.

Chapter 3

What it Takes to
Grow Psychological Safety

"Organizations are more at risk of preventable business failures or human safety failures when psychological safety is low."

— Amy Edmondson, Ph.D.

One Chief Security Officer of a publicly traded organization was so intellectually quick and assertive that he was often perceived as abrasive. This leader was also a change agent and often challenged his peers. It was difficult for him to work with peers who didn't absorb content or respond as quickly as he did to threats and new information. Over time, multiple leaders complained to the COO. The organization had a difficult time telling the CSO that he was derailing. The way we define derailment is that a person is either asked to leave a job, is made redundant and laid off, or responsibilities are taken away and their role neutralized. In some extreme examples, the company clearly hopes the leader will quit. The CSO made great strides in developing better interactions, but the damage was done. It was difficult for the senior team to see him as having changed. Better measures of how psychological safety had improved would have helped immensely. Eventually, the CSO parted ways and found himself more well-suited in an organization that was faster moving. In this case, the CSO quit and helped another healthcare organization thrive during the Covid pandemic when technology and new systems for security were critically necessary to serve patients. The CSO has since consistently grown bubbles of psychological safety early and maintained them.

Stay true to demonstrating all the principles of growing psychological safety. If you model psychological safety, you can grow it. Your resilience is paramount. It's very easy to have a bad day and slip below the line of psychological safety into promoting negativity and toxicity. That venting session you might have had that felt so cathartic may spur other people to focus on the more negative elements of a project and forget to appreciate what is working. And leaders who are too focused on creating psychological safety at the expense of focusing on job execution will actually promote toxicity. Leaders who promote toxicity by complaining about other leaders create something I affectionately like to cause the "buzz." When a leader's negative comments reach a certain volume, create complaints to senior leaders, or seem to undermine strategic priorities by questioning them too much; it's usually a matter of time before that senior leader derails. I recently told an executive who was derailing that his consistent listing of cascading problems caused by change made the senior leadership team avoid him. When he interacted with them after a change was decided, he often made others feel challenged, stupid, or that he was blocking change. Yet, I often observed he was often an early adopter of change. He simply failed to equally communicate his ownership of the change and report progress. His negativity became their focus.

Psychological safety and accountability are interdependent. Exceptional leaders honor both equally. When working with executive leadership teams I have found it helpful to urge teams to stay in the green bubble while being accountable to the many facets of their job. Too often we take a new role that is described to us in some detail. After a few short weeks, the reality of what is expected of us is typically quite different. Knowing that a person's role is constantly evolving as are the priorities at the most senior levels of an organization. It's a myth that good work in itself is enough to be successful. Anticipating that your role is going to change is only half the equation. The other half of the success equation is convincing your peers that your accountabilities need to change as well.

One regional medical director and her team were given the key priority to retain physicians during the pandemic. When patient loads fell, operational efficiency and scheduling cutbacks were necessary. Physicians began quitting when their hours were cut and they had to practice seeing patients with skeleton care teams. The regional medical director pivoted to help operations train new staff to fill care team roles and shore up the load. She realized that she needed to be accountable to making sure clinics were running smoothly and profitably. Her operations counterpart felt she was overstepping her role and constantly complained that the medical director needed to "stay in her lane." When she presented the numbers of physicians at risk of leaving and challenged operations to make some changes, it ruffled feathers. Like many leaders, the regional medical director silenced her voice. She became dissatisfied with her role. After a few months, the regional medical director moved to another medical institution and attrition of key physicians increased.

"Associations at their very core are in the relationship business. It is critical that every member of our field (in our case, hospitals) is in the association tent, and has a trusting relationship with me as CEO, and with everyone on our MHA team with whom they interact. The foundation of our historic success in this regard is the ability to first create a strong culture within our own workplace – a culture that prioritizes psychologically safe bubbles. As the CEO, I feel personally responsible for setting this standard and leading by example. We consistently talk about the "MHA Family." Among other things, this concept includes treating everyone, no matter their job title or seniority within the organization, as a valued member of our team whose insights will be valued, and whose needs both inside and outside of the office will be genuinely considered. In 2021, we were honored by Modern Healthcare as one of the Best Places to Work in Healthcare in America. I am convinced that our emphasis on this psychologically safe culture was a major contributor."

Brian Peters, Chief Executive Officer
Michigan Health & Hospital Association

Our ability to collaborate, socialize ideas, gather different perspectives is called stakeholdering. A trying trusted advisor is invaluable to a stakeholder because they know you hold them in a strong (green) bubble of psychological safety where they can be authentic, future focused, and work with you to solve complex problems holistically. Of course, your immediate team wants to live in a strong bubble of psychological safety with you. And they need to know how to be successful. What is the target? How will you bring new members up-to-speed about your pivotal priorities? See the above/below line chart in the appendix.

Anything below the line indicates that either the psychological safety bubble is fragile or accountability neglected. Leaders understand the importance of psychological safety, but few know how to:

- Measure teams & individuals

- Understand psychological safety drivers

- Train & develop leaders to improve

- Hold managers accountable

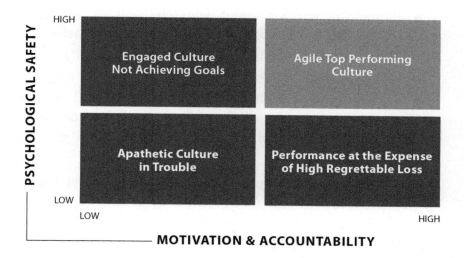

In any organization, people need to know what the 1 or 2 key priorities are. I am a big proponent of objectives and key results (OKR) or key performance indicators (KPI's) in business. Sometimes we call these big bets or pivotal priorities. For a team to have accountability, they need a strong point of view of what the goal is and constant monitoring of how well that goal is being met. By now, you have been taking a look in the mirror and examining your thoughts, assumptions and self-awareness. At this stage, you need to select a pivotal priority.

A pivotal priority is a bold point of view of something you want to change. Are you willing to prioritize this with time, budget, make sacrifices, and tradeoffs? Do you have a deep awareness of how different stakeholders will view your point of view? Are you willing to stand behind your point of view in a way that builds followership and relationships? Take action in small executable steps every day—even without all the information. Experiment until you get momentum. Then, you'll need to monitor your zone of psychological safety, leadership basics, communication, and tenacity.

- Remaining curious about yourself, seeking feedback, and setting metrics for your own performance helps you deepen your self-awareness.

- As a leader, live by the mantra that teams can't focus on everything. In one study conducted by Cornell of over 2,000 managers, researchers discovered that managers were distracted from focusing on pivotal priorities 87% of the time.[28]

- A team that understands what priorities are 'must haves', are less likely to get distracted. They need to have those pivotal priorities published, revisited, updated, and celebrated when they are accomplished.

  - One big five accounting firm partner was having trouble keeping his young team motivated on a particularly crushing audit. He took the time to have a banner printed for their main conference room showing the milestones of the audit, who was responsible, and what success would look like. As each milestone was achieved, the team celebrated. Although everyone

---

[28] Bruch, Heike, and Sumantra Ghoshal. "Beware the Busy Manager." PubMed 80, no. 2 (February 1, 2002): 62–69, 128. https://pubmed.ncbi.nlm.nih.gov/11894679.

worked long hours, they remained more resilient and anticipatory about what handoffs would be needed from one role to the next. It also allowed the team to complete work in parallel and free up personal time that would have been otherwise lost.

- We recommend you help your team identify 3-4 pivotal priorities each year.. This may lead to important trade-offs. Have open discussions with the team about what to change, keep doing, and stop doing. Where can they better spend their time, measure success, invest?

- Each day we take small executable steps toward those big bets.

Typical big bets that help a group be accountable include:

- Making changes to improve long-term financial stability
- Helping a department grow psychological safety so employees can do their best
- Launching a new educational/career offering
- Hiring an exceptional new team member even when you know it will take more effort to onboard
- Asking to have your role redefined
- Developing a new recruiting channel for team members who are diverse
- Restructuring your incentives to be more closely tied to better outcomes, collaboration, and growing a culture of psychological safety
- Initiating a new way to work with strategic partners
- Something else you are passionate about that will equally benefit your team, your organization, and the community

I encourage people to adopt the mantra, promote your mindset two levels higher than your current role. To be fully accountable, imagine what your organization needs to achieve. Can you think of accountability in terms of how the CEO will likely be measured. This also helps you define what pivotal priorities really matter. I once worked with a senior leader who admitted she had retired in place. Despite having strong relationships with the CEO and CFO, she had stopped using her strategic voice and was waiting to be fully eligible for her pension. We had the chance to go to dinner after months of feeling like I had not made any progress in our coaching. I remembered the restaurant, the wine, but not much of our conversation. She called me a few weeks later to tell me that our conversation had changed her life. I laughed and said, "well, what did I say?" She replied, "You told me to live my life like I'm not afraid of getting fired." I've carried this mantra with me (and this story) with me for almost 20 years. Sometimes the wine talks. Instead of retiring in place, she made a great impact on the company and went on to a lucrative consulting career instead of retiring.

- When you look across the entire enterprise, what problems are the senior leaders trying to solve?
- What topics are being discussed at the operating committee level?
- What changes do people think the organization needs to make to stay relevant in the future?
- Are there risks in the markets or with the people you serve that aren't getting enough air time at the top of the house?
- Are there blocks or challenges in the business/non-profit/community/region that are preventing us from serving our client base as well as you can?
- What are our senior leaders most proud of as they look at last year's successes?

Think like a Chief Executive Officer. The President and Chief Executive Officer is responsible for the overall leadership and effective management of the organization and its subsidiaries, setting the strategic direction and driving total performance consistent with the interests of shareholders, customers, employees and other stakeholders. The CEO is accountable for economic returns (or economic sustainability if you are a nonprofit).

Primary Responsibilities

- Develops for the board's approval, strategic vision and plans to ensure profitable growth and success for the organization; as well as sound capital and operating plans to meet goals and objectives as agreed to with the board.

- Embodies the values of the organization, sets the right "tone at the top," fosters a culture of integrity throughout the organization and meets the highest of ethical standards.

- Responsible for the overall risk profile, ensures the enterprise risk profile is managed within the defined risk appetite, appropriate risk diversification is in place and promotes a culture of ethical business conduct and prudent risk management.

- Ensures leadership development and succession plans are in place to provide the continuity of leadership required by the firm for the future.

- Sets an operational philosophy that is performance driven and maintains an environment of high employee engagement.

- Develops and motivates the executive leadership team, delegates authority and responsibility for strategic initiatives and individual tasks and provides overall management to ensure the leadership team is effective.

- Fosters a climate of customer focus and collaboration; develops and maintains key client relationships. Sets the tone for effective business development by leveraging the group's capabilities to bring the best to clients.

- Promotes the organization internally and externally and strengthens the brand and positive public profile of the firm. Serves as chief spokesperson for the enterprise communicating effectively with the financial and investment community, customers, shareholders, governments, regulators and other key publics.

- Acts as a final decision-maker under the board's delegation of authority and ensures all operations are conducted in full compliance with laws, regulations and the firm's code of conduct.

- Works closely with the chair of the board to facilitate effective board oversight by fostering relevant and engaged board discussions, ensuring information is made available in a timely and effective manner and the best advice and counsel are drawn from board members during meetings and as required throughout the year.

If you thought like a CEO in your organization, what pivotal priorities would rise to the surface? Take a few moments and identify your top 3 priorities for your team.

Pivotal Priority & Metrics	Psychological Safety
(What, When, Who, and To What Degree)	(How people can communicate and interact to promote all the elements of psychological safety)
1.	
2.	
3.	

In this chapter we explore the way you think drives how you behave which drives how people perceive you. Examine how you think carefully to lead well and grow psychological safety for those around you. If you are interested in seeing how your mindsets are perceived by others and to explore your own executive awareness, you might benefit from getting some feedback using the Awareness2020™—a 720° measures that shows you have the right frame of mind to lead large groups of people to achieve pivotal priorities.[29] A 720° assessment measures your progress over time to track how you are advancing and growing.

In an environment like the private equity industry that is intense, incredibly competitive and operates in a constantly changing macroeconomic landscape, creating psychologically safe spaces is a differentiator. When the implications of mistakes or of missed opportunities can literally mean the success or failure of an enterprise, making team members feel valued and safe can drive loyalty and enhanced results. People who feel they belong are more willing to take calculated risks, think more creatively about solving problems and build or deepen the relationships that are crucial to get a deal across the finish line. Taking fear or uncertainty out of the workplace allows people to better focus on leveraging their full skill set and perspective to win, in private equity and in any business environment.

Carmen Ortiz-McGhee | Chief Operating Officer
National Association of Investment Companies

---

[29] Executive Core, Singer Barbara, and Dorothy Siminovitch. "Awareness2020." Executivecore.com. Executive Core, 2018. Accessed November 21, 2023. https://executivecore.com.

Mindsets to Help you Lead from a Psychologically Safe Bubble

To lead from an umbrella of psychological safety, you need to have disciplined thinking that helps you stay centered, resilient, optimistic in times of strife, and driven. Performance mindsets, similar to the ones that Olympic athletes use, keep you focused on ambitious and consistent levels of excellence.

It all starts with how you think. Cogita ergo sum. Je pense, doc je suis. I think, therefore I am. Rene Descartes reminded us we are sentient beings. In this world of artificial intelligence, it matters more than ever that we know how important our thoughts are lest you let someone else do the thinking for you. I like to turn off the navigation system in my car and make my teenage children figure out how to get somewhere. We also teach our children to navigate our regional waters in the Great Lakes by navigational markers, landmarks, and compass direction. When they hike, they carry a compass and still occasionally look at maps online—but at least they are looking. Sometimes we get a little lost but the adventure we have along the way is worth it.

As we approach a new phase of human existence defined by the information age and AI, most futurists predict that repetitive tasks will be eliminated—anything that can be understood using an algorithm will be automated using technology. Yet, the fundamentals of humanity in the workplace remain the same. Our ability to act with wisdom, sensitivity to others, and self-awareness remains one of the best predictors of leadership success. We still need our humanity. We need equal amounts of head and heart. Our careers and our happiness depend on how we think. Too often we get distracted and forget to examine our own thoughts.

Consider that the average person spends their life in the following way.[30]

- 12,000 average days at work
- 35,000 decisions each day
- Up to 60 hours a month wasted at work (estimates simply based on how much an average employee surfs the internet for personal reasons during working hours)
- 87% of employees distracted from priorities[31]
- Nearly every human demonstrates some kind of leadership trait (1 in a million do not) yet most fail to influence
- Change is all around us
- Figuring out what and who to focus on is our biggest challenge

In 2019, my colleague Dorothy Simonvitch, PhD and I completed a body of research on executive awareness and developed a 720° feedback online survey.[32] For decades, clients had been approaching us asking to help leaders develop "executive presence." When we asked clients specifically what executive presence meant to them the responses were highly varied. We decided to begin our journey to quantify what that meant. Dorothy's work in Gestalt psychology and my work in predictors of executive success and executive integral leadership, led us to focus on how leaders think matters greatly.

---

[30] Kouzes, Jim and Association of Corporate Executive Coaches. "Everyday People, Extraordinary Leadership." Slide show. https://acec-conference.org/award-recipients, n.d.
[31] Bruch and Ghoshal, "Beware the Busy Manager."
[32] Executive Core, Barbara, and Siminovitch, "Awareness2020."

Awareness can be defined as the act of being cognizant to both your inner self, other people, and the outside world. Self-awareness has been studied for decades and shown to be a critical success factor for leaders. The amount of information and change facing leaders today is increasing rapidly so remaining fully aware is becoming more difficult.

The development of our tool began with a comprehensive review of the literature and what emerged included seven awareness dimensions. Our pilot study was conducted, which involved collecting Awareness 20/20 data on 26 leaders from 218 stakeholders, including their peers, subordinates, managers, and others (e.g., customers). We were pleased that our instrument surpassed standards of reliability, but more importantly they grew to help us help observe leaders evolve how they think to a more holistic perspective. The tool helps increase leaders' self-awareness, ability to connect with others, and leadership effectiveness. We have continued to make these performance mindsets an integral part of building bubbles of psychological safety. One executive who had not invested enough time in his own self-awareness found the mindsets to be a useful guide.

> "I have profoundly changed into an aware leader that acts with compassion, values, and passion towards not just the projects, but also with the team who is committed to making an impact. I started actively listening to the people by being present without multi-tasking. I elevated myself over negativity and fostered coaching and collaboration in my everyday work environment by not micromanaging. I lead by a defined set of values to be a force of good to the employees that report to me, to the family that depends on me, and to the friends, colleagues, and classmates that inspire me. In the future, people will say that I am transformed into a

kind, humble, feedback oriented, dependable, plai
and focused individual that values integrity and works
for greater meaning in life."

When you exhibit high levels of awareness, people tend to experience us as sincere, having high integrity, and trust us. Humans' struggle with self-awareness is timeless and woven throughout the writings of all cultures. If you combine deep awareness with constantly acquiring new knowledge, you will likely excel at thinking in complex, systemic, strategic, and interdependent ways. A fully aware leader managing complex organizations requires a high IQ, Awareness quotient, and high relationship quotient. People tend to follow leaders who have these attributes[33].

Adhere to High Ethics

MINDSET CHALLENGE:

Focus on the higher good. Consistently remind yourself that, "In even the smallest acts and decisions, I can leave people and places better than I found them."

As of today, many sources are tracking the growth of "social entrepreneurship," people investing in businesses that seek to drive specific social change or provide broad social, cultural, or environmental benefits. Global progress in reducing extreme poverty has been made in part by "investments in people's education, health, and social safety nets," and prominent CEOs are committing to the United Nations Sustainable Development Goals. One leader wrote, "By Leadership, I am learning to look through the eyes of a CEO with a challenge of making smart business decisions today, that make tomorrow a better place for all humanity."

Ask yourself how you define the greater collective good. Identify something you are passionate about and work toward goals that benefit teams, organizations, society, nature. A new organizational scorecard that has growing relevance is the Triple Bottomline (TBL) and consists of three P's: profit, people, and the planet. It aims to measure the financial, social and environmental performance of the corporation over a period of time. Only a company that produces a TBL is taking account of the full cost involved in doing business. Great leaders are increasingly defined as those who understand that they need to be connected to the greater purpose that business serves.

- Another helpful way to approach this dimension is to articulate your ideas as they relate to your entire organization. What decision is best for the entire organization? The people we serve? Our communities? Our environment

- Don't confuse this dimension with religion. Much has been written to suggest that a tolerant society that encourages people to focus on the greater good and universal virtues leads to happier societies.

- Today John Muir is best remembered for his writing, but during his life Muir was an inspirational speaker as well. Largely because of a series of articles that Muir wrote and his inspirational appeals to the American people about preserving shared natural spaces for future generations; in 1890 Yosemite became a national park. In 1892, he founded the Sierra Club that continues to lobby for conservation issues today. In his lifetime Muir was able to touch millions of Americans and launch the environmental movement.[34]

---

[34] Singer, Barbara and Lore International. Personal Influence. 2nd ed. Awareworks, 2004.

- Appealing to other people's values can be an extremely effective way to influence. Your values should be consistent with the message you are sending. And your message should also relate directly to the other person's values.

- Find out how your values relate to the values of others around you. People you think are extremely different may surprise you by sharing similar values. And appealing to values is a great way to be a force for good.

- Look around for opportunities to help someone before they ask. I ask my children to enter a room when they are guests and look to see what small chore they could do to help. It might be picking up a dirty dish or putting away a toy. In our organizations we can adopt the same mindset. "What can look around and see what needs to be done before anyone asks."

After collecting hundreds of gratitude journals from executive MBA students, most leaders are grateful for their loved ones, trusted colleagues, their homes, moments to reflect or stretch their legs, acts of kindness, and simply taking a moment to be aware of the beauty around them. You can almost hear their voices as you read their what they are most grateful for:

Hear Mom's voice
Going to Second City
Affording a nice meal in a nice restaurant
Family safe after bad weather in NOLA
New friends, old friends
Meals delivered to your door
Help from co-workers
A good workout
Safe flights, and a good luggage handler!

Keep reminding yourself to live life with gratitude. Remember to promote your mindset two levels higher than your current role. One leader wrote to me that he appreciated my challenge to "go big" and ask the higher level question. He wrote,

> *"While I have always been known to be someone who "goes big", I realized that I do not do that all the time. "Going big," even when it matters more to someone else than it does to me, will significantly improve how I impact others around me. Taking the time to step out of the situation and look back has enabled me to ask the higher-level question. Ultimately this leads to a more holistic look at a problem, all the while striking at the core of that problem. When you do this, you can see both people and business problems more holistically."*

Michael Carroll was an extraordinary student in the Notre Dame Executive MBA program. Michael showed up to class in a 10 gallon cowboy hat, boots, with a Texas drawl. He exuded both charisma and warmth. He was quick witted and likely to zero in on a clever strategy to help a company turnaround. As CEO of his real estate development company, Michael enjoyed a sideline helping a best friend from NYU's school of film produce movies. I remember watching one of the movies he helped produce called "Drunk Bus," a heartwarming tale of a college graduate trying to jumpstart his career while still driving the college late bus home from the bars. When Michael was passionate about something or someone, he committed himself. On one of the first days of the program, Michael challenged the class to "show the fuck up" to make the most of the graduate experience. He later wrote me his mission statement.

> *"I WILL "SHOW UP" by proactively offering available opportunities, through my resources and contacts, to pro- mote the well-being of my EMBA cohort so it will go and do good in business. I now know being a leader involves*

understanding intimately the priorities of my class and I will try to make them my own, not just cognitively but spiritually. Integrating our individual but shared values, woven into a common thread as a class, I will strive to be honest, open and candid in my intentions and communications with my classmates through cognitive spiritual reflection and cooperative execution throughout this program. By the end of the EMBA, my classmates will say that they found me reliable and I showed the F$%K up to promote them within and outside the program!"

Michael did just that. He led the class in spirit and intellect until he tragically died of an aneurysm during the program. Michael lived life large and inspired us all. While his death broke our hearts, his spirit lives on in the faculty and students that shared his journey. Later I had the honor of meeting his siblings who were donating a trust to fund an annual scholarship in Michael's honor. I was grateful I could tell them a few riveting stories of Michael's antics and relationships before he died. Today I keep a rosary and memoir on my office shelf to remind me to "show the fuck up." We don't know how long our lives will be. Instead of letting life's trivial frustrations get us mentally stuck, Michael would have wanted us to go Texas big.

In one assessment I conducted for a Fortune 50 company's top 500 leaders, only 2% were considered skilled at leading people internally, externally, and operationally. Enterprise leaders are rare. Consider how you develop your leadership internally, externally, and work towards operational excellence.

If you could stop chasing the level and the role; how would you chase what you haven't already done? Enterprise leaders have a systems mindset. They can take on the perspective of all the major functions of their organization, customers, strategic partners, suppliers, and competitors. They are rare. People who think systematically are willing to sacrifice and make trade-offs for the

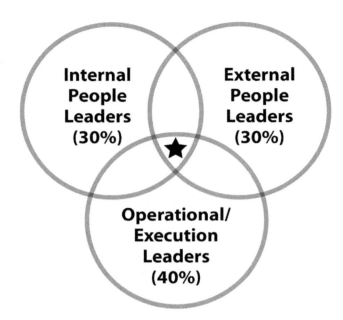

good of other parts of the organization. They can also look around the corner and better anticipate market trends. Finally, they understand the ripple effect of decisions both in a short-term and long-term way. We always encourage leaders we know to do things you haven't done before and to get a well-rounded experience set of the entire organization. At a minimum, understand what your customers/clients/constituents/communities need, understand the financials of your organization, and know how to grow markets/footprint profitability.

Make an Impact: Live your career like you are not afraid of getting fired

How do you make an impact?

1. Achieve positive success outside of the organization
2. Improve internally (especially across functions holistically)

3. Positively impact your work team
4. Help others come up with new ideas
5. Help individuals with their careers
6. Make an impact beyond the enterprise in the industry/ society

Working with high potential senior women at Royal Bank of Canada for 10 years, I have been constantly impressed with their dedication to make an impact both within the bank and their communities. It's not unusual for me to read biographies of leaders who have passages like:

With over 15 years of international experience, she has worked and lived in several cities including Washington, London, Dubai, Hong Kong, Geneva, Toronto, New York and Montreal.

Currently co-founder and head of Arrive, a digital platform designed to help newcomers access the information and assistance they need to make a smoother transition to Canada. Arrive is one of the first organic ventures built in-house at RBC Ventures, an accelerator that's focused on identifying and investing in opportunities to go beyond banking.

Senior Director of Anti-Money Laundering: Leading a team in Canadian Banking Compliance that built out enhanced Monitoring and Testing oversight. Her strong performance has consistently been recognized and is well illustrated by the RBC Gold Award and two-time RBC Performance Conference she has received.

Mother of two and just finished a bike ride across Canada to raise money for underserved youth.

Integrity requires more than words. It requires action. People expect to see your results and that you achieved them with dignity, kindness, and grace.

Is Authentic

MINDSET CHALLENGE:

Deepen your Self Awareness. Consistently remind yourself that, "I have boundless curiosity about myself, how to be my best, with compassion and clarity regarding how others see me."

Authenticity and deep self-awareness go hand in hand. A leader who knows when and how to be truthful about themself, while keeping a sense of levity and even humor, wins hearts.

Consider your own mindset, which refers to how you make meaning. Think of a moment when you lacked awareness about something. Perhaps you wanted to explain a piece of valid feedback or were simply unsure of how to see yourself. Perhaps you were harder on yourself than others. Try to pinpoint what you were thinking. See if you can replace that assumption with something more helpful. One executive wrote, "The key business problem I started with is how does the bank get our customers (banks, credit unions, etc.) to borrow money from us when they are flush with deposits and don't need the funds. My biggest problem is that I need to relax and stop worrying so much about failing or looking bad. This obsession is pervasive in everything I do. I worry about my direct reports not doing something right, about looking dumb. it is okay if some of those ideas don't work. I left inspired and truly impressed. I also left with that same goal of granting more autonomy to my staff."

You are likely in a zone of better self-awareness when:

- You see yourself, team members, and the situation at work accurately
- You don't lose site of the end goal and remind people positively of what they are working toward
- Your strong sense of self exudes confidence and thoughtfulness. People at all levels in the organization will want to hear what you have to say.
- You can consistently articulate to others both your strengths and your opportunities for growth
- Highly self-aware leaders are seen as consistent. If your behavior, words, tone, or nonverbal signals do not match what people expect, then relationships, followership, and even credibility can be negatively impacted.

Ways to be seen as more consistent:

- Ask for written feedback after a presentation, and scan it for discrepancies between what you thought you were saying and what your audience heard.
- Have a trusted colleague use a smartphone to video you making a presentation or running a meeting, and review it with other trusted colleagues for gaps between self-perception and visual documentation.
- Create an operating manual that tells your employees how you want to receive information and how you reach decisions. Share with your employees how you typically respond to stress, and what you're doing to stay resilient under high-stress situations. If you're unable to stay centered, consider outside help or increased physical activity to keep you on a more even keel.

- Articulate your intentions early and often. To reassure people that they are psychologically safe, encourage debate, and be sure that everyone is heard and respected, even if their ideas are not pervasively held.

- Openly acknowledge and explain any changes in your usual behavior.

- Highly self-aware leaders connect and communicate with others. They simultaneously appreciate the past, clearly perceive the current situation, and can imagine and articulate a positive future direction. They have a long-term vision that they communicate clearly, so that others understand it. These leaders are open to and absorb new information that influences their change strategies, so they invite others into their decision-making processes. See if you might fine-tune your resources and how you communicate your knowledge and vision to others.

Ways to show you are connected:

- Talk about people's roles and responsibilities and appreciate how each person provides valuable contributions.

- Share why you are passionate about what you do and about what people around you do. If you are not "passionate," then what parts of your job or role do you really enjoy? If you are burned out, people likely perceive you as disconnected. Work with a trusted advisor to arrange a brief time-out or to implement a strategy to recharge.

- If people think you are aloof, take some time to make your thinking more explicit. Share how you feel about things that are relevant or important to them.

- Highly self-aware leaders demonstrate that they are comfortable in their role. If you exhibit disinterest in or disconnection from your assigned role, people will notice, and your work may be undermined. Take time to articulate to others why you are suited for your position, and how you see others' contributions as valuable to the group.

- Staying Engaged
- Gallup, the research and polling institution, estimates that actively disengaged employees cost the world $8.8 Trillion each year in lost productivity.[35] Think through how well you help your colleagues, your direct reports, and even your senior leaders sustain their commitment and energy. Are there other ways to support yourself and others in making more satisfactory and more productive use of their time? You might, for example, consider eliminating low-value activities that do not meaningfully contribute to employees' engagement or to key priorities.

One leader in news media sent this summary of his experience:

"Expect me to show up, actively listen and take time to stop and look at the big picture. I will embrace the business rationale, establish clear goals, and communicate a vision. I will be present with my family and my colleagues, striving for quality not quantity. I will never forget that all people are broken, to treat them with the kindness and respect they deserve, not to rush to judgment. I will strive each day to be an enhanced and more fulfilled version of the person I was the day before."

Is Willing to Discuss Tough Issues

Communication is at the heart of psychological safety. I often counsel teams to give feedback in a 3:1 ratio. Appreciate what team

---

[35] Gallup, and Ryan Wendell. "Employee Engagement Strategies: Fixing the World's $8.8 Trillion Problem." *Workplace*, September 11, 2023. https://www.gallup.com/workplace/393497/world-trillion-workplace-problem.aspx.

members are doing well to meet and achieve their pivotal priorities 3 x to every once you make an observation, explain the impact it is having, and provide a suggestion/question to help the person discover new possibilities or prevent unfavorable outcomes.

MINDSET CHALLENGE:

Discussing tough issues requires patience and tenacity. Consistently remind yourself that, "If first I don't succeed in communicating with another person or group, instead of simply trying harder, I can try something different. How others want to be communicated with may be different than how and when I prefer to communicate."

In the words of one leader,

> *"As a Technical leader at Rolls-Royce, my leadership style used to take a passive approach versus an active approach; I now know that one cannot exist without the other. While my teams appreciate the freedom, they can often get frustrated by the lack of structure and direction required for an appropriately scoped deliverable. I came to the realization that one of the reasons I focus on the passive approach is because I often feel as though I do not have the qualifications to lead a technical engineering team. I have found more strength and confidence in myself to know when and how to communicate."*

Awareness of how to gather relevant information and effectively share it with others is at the heart of leadership. The ability to find an appropriate balance between listening and asserting is a predictor of leadership success.

If you would like to increase your communication awareness, consider how well you time your communication so others are likely to hear it. If another person is distracted, upset, or focused on a bigger priority; they may not be receptive to your message. Earlier in the book, I mentioned Richard Okello, who was working for the Mayor of Indianapolis at the time this book was published. Richard was in charge of citizen complaints in police altercations. Indianapolis, as one of the most violent cities in the country, experiences strong tensions between the black community during routine police pullovers. Since George Floyd's murder, Richard has been advocating with citizen groups like the Urban League how to navigate their rights but had been challenged in presentations that he didn't understand despite being a black man himself. He and I puzzled over how to connect with neighborhood leaders who were already worn down and angry. Richard helped me to think even further about applications for psychological safety. Anti-hate movements around the country are rising. Communities like ADL, the Urban League, and The Asian American Foundation are raising the awareness of the need for both physical and psychological safety in our communities. How could you apply these concepts in your own backyard? Richard and I worked together to brainstorm how psychological safety might decrease tension during routine police stops. Richard changed his presentation to admit that he did not grow up in the underserved, predominantly black neighborhoods of Indianapolis and that he expected people in the audience not to trust him and think of him as an outsider. His authentic declaration deescalated the friction often projected on him when speaking on the topic. Richard has been presenting to the community to begin each pull-over with the phrase, "I want you safe. I want me safe. How do we go about doing that." Simple. Powerful.

Consider your level of adaptability. Most of us get stuck communicating more often in one of the following patterns:

1. Overly assertive at the expense of showing others that you are both interested and sensitive to their feelings. In this case you might benefit from practicing asking

more questions and demonstrating that you can take the perspective of the other person.

2. More listening than asserting at the expense of not highlighting your best ideas. In this case, you might make your thoughts and ideas explicit at the beginning of a conversation and then ask the other person to expand your ideas to make them even better. After sharing your ideas, ask what else is important that you might not have considered.

3. Some leaders find they simply detach and do not assert or listen as much as their colleagues want/need. If you've detached, stopped communicating, and find yourself doing projects on your own, consider the cost. You may be getting tasks done but failing to develop followership.

A lot of listening and a lot of asserting puts you in the most ideal zone to co-build ideas and solutions with other people. People who can both assert and listen tend to have the highest scores in this dimension. Cultural norms play a large role in how people express themselves and what others find attractive. Understand your own operating style (you might try taking the MBTI®, Hogan®, or Disc® to better understand yourself). Learn how to see operating styles of others, and their cultural influences in order to adapt your message.

Consider mastering the following three styles: consulting, coaching, and asserting[36]:

> **Consulting** is defined as, "Incorporating another's ideas into your request or co-building a solution with another party." People appreciate when you appeal to their experience and ideas. Be sure to also share your

---

[36] Executive Core and Singer, *Psychological Safety and the Languages of Influence.*

ideas and co-build solutions together. You might say something like, "I've outlined three different ways to approach this. In your experience, what might work the best?"

Asserting is asking for what you want clearly. If someone does not know what you want them to do or know, they may not prioritize what you are communicating. They might become distracted. They might even become frustrated as time is precious. Try to state a shared goal you have with another person in 10 words or less. Then, state clearly what you want them to do/know in 10 words or less. Ironically fewer words mean there is less chance for misinterpretation and people understand what you want faster. For instance, "Growing this part of the business is important. We need to invest more time selling."

Coaching is a way of communicating with another person to help discover their creative strategies toward goal attainment. When you help a person succeed, they tend to be more open and trusting of your communication. You can also help shape the way they accomplish tasks and build stronger relationships with other team members. Consider asking a person what they want to achieve. What are their goals? What do they need to change? What's holding them back? What else is important? Remind others to focus on what they can control when you are coaching. This helps the other person avoid negativity and focus on their own behaviors. Effective communicators are courageous when sharing observations, insights, and encouragement with others. A great coach also takes the time to gather accurate information to ensure they have a full understanding of the person's situation.

Experiment with all three communication styles to improve your effectiveness.

Refrains from Intellectual Bullying

"I don't suffer fools gladly."

"I get impatient in meetings when people don't want to change."

"I know I have to give people time to absorb the information, but I just wish they could process information faster."

"People are bureaucratic, stuck in their ways, and would rather wait to get direction from senior leaders than see solutions for themselves."

"They are retired in place."

"He is quietly quitting, and I don't have time for that."

"I inherited people who underperform. I just wish I could hire a brand new more talented/experienced/motivated team."

"If I don't question their solution, they are not going to anticipate the roadblocks."

"I'm not really resistant to change. I just ask questions to challenge how we are going to accomplish this. The leader hasn't thought it through."

"She's the smartest person I know."

Chances are if you've had feedback about any of the above statements, you might have damaged your psychological safety bubble. Refraining from being intellectually intimidating requires great emotional intelligence. We often say a psychological safe leadership bubble requires a high awareness quotient, high relationship quotient, high intelligence quotient, and high emotional intelligence quotient. Perhaps the most important of the list to preventing intellectual intimidation is an emotional quotient. My youngest son has a love of Greek and Roman mythology. He recently recounted a tale of Hercule's problem with his first wife. While we often think of Hercules as a hero who got results, my young son commented, "they might have been gods or demigods, but the Greek and Roman Gods were often real jerks." As the myth goes, Hercules killed his children after a fit of rage where he lacked emotional, relationship, and intelligence quotients.

MINDSET CHALLENGE:

Emotional intelligence keeps us level-headed without ignoring emotions. Consistently remind yourself that, "I trust that my emotions are a valid source of information and that optimistic thinking and appreciation the emotional states or others can drive happiness and success, even in the face of failure."

After traveling to West Chester, New York to work with a group of Egon Zehnder partners I noticed one of the European leaders wearing the same clothes for the third day in a row. The hotel where we were meeting was renovating the rooms. After the first day of meetings the partner returned to his room and noticed that his hotel furniture had been changed. A fastidious and organized executive, he had promptly unpacked all of his clothes into the dressers on the first day. By day two, there was no trace of a stitch of clothing except what he was wearing. When he inquired at the front desk, he was told the furniture had been taken to the city and auctioned off that same day. All of his clothes for the week had gone to auction with the furniture. Instead of showing the least bit of irritation, he had the entire room doubled over in laughter as he recounted the story. To this day, I rarely unpack my clothes beyond the hotel closet and my suitcase, and I always chuckle as I remember his good humor at the situation.

Leaders who have strong emotional intelligence (EI) tend to be those people who recognize and understand their emotions while also being able recognize and respond to other peoples' emotions. EI is defined as the "ability to monitor one's emotions while using this information to guide one's thinking and actions." Emotionally intelligent leaders demonstrate strength and the capacity to recover from hopelessness, fear, frustration, and aimless anxiety. Being able to recognize what others are feeling serves as a professional, social, and personal asset. Because these leaders recognize how emotions, whether negative or positive, can be contagious to others, they look to offer humor and a range of positive emotions such as joy, gratitude, and happiness, which strengthens the working environment. One leader writes, "to become a better project manager I need to become more decisive and remove my assumption *'if I'm direct with someone they won't like me anymore.'* During meetings at work, I remind myself that if I deliver results and am confident in my decisions that I will earn trust from my peers and managers. This strategic focus and decisiveness has already helped my team start achieving better results in our company's largest initiative, growing our footprint with oncology practices."

- Pay attention to the frequency of your negative emotions, since negative emotions can contribute to a negative work environment. One simple but powerful way to reduce and manage negative emotions is to practice "steady breathing" immediately upon experiencing a negative emotion. Begin by intentionally inhaling for 4 seconds, then exhaling for 5 seconds. After 4-5 breaths like this, a relaxation response gets stimulated, and you will feel calmer and less negative. With practice you can feel this shift after just a few breaths. This simple practice is regularly reported as helping people move from reactivity to better emotional control. You can practice this behavior whenever you need to shift from negative emotions.

- You can benefit from learning to recognize your feelings by getting curious about strong feelings when they occur around important issues. One easy practice to better recognize your feelings is to "name" your strong feeling and to ask, "What is this feeling about?" Recognition of what triggers strong emotions allows you to move from reactivity to more disciplined self-control, which will raise your emotional intelligence thus preventing you from begin derailed by emotional activity and contributing to better decision-making.

- Mindful practice" is a growing activity among people in the workplace. Mindfulness has best been defined as "paying attention . . . on purpose, in the present moment, and non-judgmentally." Can you practice paying attention to your own emotions, and to the strong emotions you observe in others, with mindfulness and curiosity, without judgment? If so, you'll notice over time that you can inspire more acceptance, interest, and engagement from others.

- The ability to understand people well is connected to being able to recognize the emotions other people demonstrate. One way to recognize what people are feeling is to check their facial expressions. There are seven universal emotions that can be discerned in everyone through brief facial expressions: anger, fear, sadness, disgust, contempt, surprise, and happiness. Train yourself to recognize each.

- Key decision-makers and high potential leaders find the ability to accurately differentiate among emotions helps them respond more appropriately, especially in sensitive, high-risk situations and work-related experiences. Fear, for example, carries a message that something is wrong, but it emerges as an emotion before it is a thought. If we can recognize and name the fear being expressed, we can act on its message in wiser, more productive ways.

- The practice of verbal appreciation and validation has gained a lot of notice as being one of the most direct ways to inspire a positive emotional tone between yourself and others. Practice expressing verbal recognition and appreciation to colleagues, peers, and subordinates when even the smallest of tasks has been successfully accomplished.

- Make a commitment to learn from failure, which we define as occurring when expectations are not met. Make an agreement with yourself to use failure as a learning experience, and to use the accompanying emotions as signals to help you do better in the future. Taking care of your health and stress level will help you become more adaptive and resilient.

Creates an Enjoyable Atmosphere

During Covid, one leader who always makes me smile, was living alone in a city apartment. To liven up team meetings, he introduced a video spoof of MTV Cribs. By composing music, dancing, and dressing up; he entertained the team on the first scheduled Zoom with his Crib tour. Each meeting another person would take a personal risk to be funny and give their most entertaining tour of their home office and weird corners of their home. Today, this leader remains a manbassador for attracting diverse talent, inspiring start-up founders, and generally lighting up just about every room he enters.

If you can only select one performance mindset to help grow psychological safety, being creative is fun. For most leaders, their stakeholders rate them as average in this area. People are happiest when they are learning. A little bit of stress defends against depression. Too much unprocessed stress leads to burnout. If you keep a creative mindset, creating an enjoyable atmosphere is far more likely to follow.

MINDSET CHALLENGE:

Creating an enjoyable atmosphere requires some creativity. Consistently remind yourself that, "I get energized from discovering new possibilities and that the world needs new ideas as a natural part of evolution."

Creative people tend to have an optimistic perspective on life. They often see the world as an abundant place full of possibilities. They tend to look for possibilities and challenges, instead of feeling discouraged by problems facing them. They stay energized during unfamiliar situations and demonstrate persistence to continue to explore new ways to accomplish tasks in a way that positively impacts people and the bottom line. They also remain open to others' ideas. They encourage creative idea generation, one idea building upon the next. Try to adopt the mindset that people do not want to be changed but that they benefit from adapting to change.

If your creativity is low, consider your environment and situation. If the environment is in crisis or in a major stressful transition; you might be suppressing creativity by worrying. If so, try to focus on things you can control and articulate what you are grateful for. Some students of mine have kept gratitude journals for 45 days and include images and photos of the things in their lives they are most grateful for. This exercise, along with random acts of kindness, fosters a sense of playfulness and fun and deep satisfaction in some areas of your life whereas not all areas may be optimal.

- Make sure you are not running on extreme exhaustion. Creativity doesn't flourish when you don't have enough sleep. Ironically, your brain's processing ability may help you come up with new ideas while you sleep. Keep a journal by your bed to jot down novel ideas and insights.

- Encourage open communication and avoid "closed doors" in the workplace. When people fail to get interesting ideas from across a wide array of perspectives, they often fail to get some interesting perspectives which lowers creativity, therefore practice being more open to new ideas.

- Look internally for solutions, especially with individual contributors and mid-level managers in an organization. Some people call these change agents the magic middle.

- Adopt the mindset of intense curiosity and explore ideas from unusual sources.

- Adopt a pattern of working that allows you and others to reframe, improvise, communicate, and value creative contributions. Learned optimism has power over despair. Like British Air and Disney, find things that have been classified as problems and turn them into opportunities. British Air reframed their team's thinking about "lost luggage" to work on an initiative to "create amazing arrival experiences" among customers. Disney took their "too long lines" and reinvented them to be part of the total Disney "experience." What can you reframe for your organization in a more positive way to rethink how you operate?

- Don't forget to be creative about how you work with people so that they remain energized, as well as how you can remain creative about work outputs.

- Reduce penalties for failing or making mistakes, especially in communication as people are sharing ideas. A pattern of suggesting that an idea "won't work," "is stupid," is "not well-researched, " or that "we've done that before" likely will lower your creativity. Reframe this pattern with curiosity, and appreciation.

- Without violating ethical regulations in your industry or area, think about how you and your team can work outside the boundaries. John Cleese, a member of the Monty Python comedy troupe, has said, "Creativity is not a talent. It is a way of operating." He emphasizes that creativity is not an inborn gift, but a cultivated ability to allow oneself to "play"—to play, especially, with ideas and norms and standards.

- Complete the sentence, I will be most proud of in 20____, when I _____?

- If you were to promote your mindset two levels higher, what kind of ideas and priorities would you be expected to creatively make?

In our work at Executive Core, we encourage people to seek out radical creativity. **What Is Radical Creativity?**

Radical creativity is the generation of new and original ideas.[37]

When we leverage differences, we discover radically creative approaches. It was documented and discussed on National Public Radio that NBC Film had passed on the rights of the movie, *Crazy Rich Asians*. NBC Film failed to estimate the power of the Asian American community in their demographic largely because they had very few AAPI executive leaders. Radical creativity thrives on diversity. Radical creativity also thrives in an environment that sets individuals free to pursue their passion. Radical creativity

---

[37] Van Dyne, Linn, Karen A. Jehn, and Ann Cummings. "Differential Effects of Strain on Two Forms of Work Performance: Individual Employee Sales and Creativity." Journal of Organizational Behavior, December 12, 2001.

is different than incremental creativity. It means people work together to do something that has not been done before.

Radical Creativity Requires

- A willingness to take risks
- Resources for creativity
- Devotion to one's career
- Creative coworkers all working together in a spirit of trust and psychological safety
- Intense curiosity about different perspectives/interests
- A voice to share new ideas
- Senior leaders who ensure that the right resources are made available

Radical vs Incremental Creativity

Most experiences focus on incremental creativity. Incremental creativity isn't bad, it just isn't radical. It makes small changes to improve performance and impacts the bottom line in small ways.

A classic test of creativity, the Torrance Test of Creative Thinking was introduced by psychologist Ellis Paul Torrance in the sixties as a way to administer a more creatively inclined IQ test[38]. Respondents were given images like a large backward checkmark and asked to finish the picture. I have had people do this exercise and their creativity has generated mountain scenes, ski jumps, ocean creatures, and more. Stimulate your own creativity by sketching a backwards checkmark and finishing your own picture.

---

[38] Torrance, E. Paul. "Torrance Tests of Creative Thinking." Data set. PsycTESTS Dataset, July 9, 2012. https://doi.org/10.1037/t05532-000.

Is Sensitive to Other's Feelings

Very few things harm feelings of psychological safety than when people's feelings are ignored or overlooked. A leader who grows a strong bubble of psychological safety requires a mindset of caring and connection. Helping your entire team be more sensitive to feelings without losing their edge to be accountable to key performance indicators (KPI's also known as objectives & key results or OKR's) is an artform.[39] Create alignment and excitement about what success is and how you will measure it.

MINDSET CHALLENGE:

Identify times when it is difficult to show caring and connection to others. Consistently remind yourself that, "I know that showing others deep compassion and acts of caring, even if it may not be reciprocated, will provide me with more opportunities to work effectively with others. I know people remember how I make them feel long after we are together."

- Caring and connection involves being aware of opportunities to approach others with the intention of strengthening relationships. Demonstrating respect, interest, compassion, and empathy fosters understanding and trust.

- Consider your usual responses to others. Most people fall into one of several patterns. Some try to please and take care of others at the expense of their own needs and wants. Some pursue their own interests at the expense of others'. Some keep others at a distance so as not to risk any breach of trust or to maintain the ability to think

---

[39] John, Doerr. Measure What Matters. New York, United States of America: Portfolio/Penguin, 2018.

independently. Finding a productive balance of respect, care, and compassion for oneself and for others is critical.

- People who are consistently rated as having high integrity (usually among their top 10 skills) are often people who also demonstrate caring and connection that others find believable and genuine. People who have a very strong sense of their own ethics and values are often those who are also most curious about and open to diverse perspectives of others.

- Understand how your colleagues, peers, and subordinates can benefit from what is important to you.

- Be curious about others' doubts or concerns.

- Ask the people around you at work how they define career success. This sends a message that you care. Offer support wherever you can when appropriate.

- It's especially important to invite feedback from those who may have a different point of view. This may increase your understanding of a complex issue while supporting an environment that encourages sharing. It also fosters a sense of trust and belonging. Invite people from diverse roles to participate in important decision-making processes, including those who are senior to you, those who are your peers, and those who are junior to you. Can you also include people who may usually be left out or overlooked?

- Is building community and relationships central to your work focus? If you view people who invite collaboration or debate as weak or unsure, consider reframing this mindset.

- If you have been given feedback, reflect on what has been offered and the insights you can derive from it. Try out the interesting new behaviors that are outside your normal skill or comfort zones.

- It is always somewhat risky for the person giving the feedback. Remember to thank people for sharing their feedback with you since their feedback reveals what they are paying attention to.

If you would like to increase your ability to show caring and connection with others, consider these steps:

- Practice reflecting the feelings of others. Acknowledge emotional expressions by pausing a bit longer before responding, projecting warmth and encouragement for people to continue, if they wish. This may be difficult for you to do if you are more comfortable with analysis and problem-solving. But sometimes people simply want you to listen and to acknowledge how they feel.

- Listen more and interrupt less. Wait for speakers to finish. Practice finding value in ideas offered.

- Acknowledge what was said, and see if you can build from them by saying, "Yes . . . and?"

- Sometimes, you do have to put another's needs before your own in order to nurture that individual's career development. How often and how well do you do this?

- Doing what's right is subjective. If something tried isn't successful, try something different. Challenge your assumptions about what leaders "should" or "should not" do.

One leader who grew to become a pioneer in accelerating diversity in business and higher education wrote early in his career,

> *"When people hear stories of my upbringing, they are inclined to praise me for "beating the odds" and typically proceed to tell me how proud they are of me. Yet for me, when people make those kinds of statements it suggests that people like me aren't supposed to be where I am,*

while I believe people like me are designed to be great. Because of this I have approached business and education with a chip on my shoulder. It always made it a point to express who I was and where I was from to prove them all wrong." Later when he had challenged his assumptions he then reflected, "As a leader I will show up very different than when I first arrived. I'd like to think that I am distinctively different already. As a leader, first and foremost I will show up. This means being confident in myself because I am prepared, passionate, and have earned everything that I have received. By the end of this team experience I feel that my peers will recognize changes to my tone, use of strategy, and my skills to creatively solve problems. My tone will change because I will empower them to be the best they can be as a person as well as a professional. My use of strategy will afford me varied perspectives to make sound decisions that can be trusted and validated. My creativity in solving problems will be evident in the manner in which we arrive at answers."

Today he has become a leading force in the U.S. to connect people of all backgrounds and skin colors. While a dedicated democrat and black leader, he has a best friend from a completely opposite economic background, Italian heritage, and political affiliation. When his friend was serving in the White House during the Trump administration, their friendship deepened and their hearts remained open. Today, I am proud to call him my friend, also.

Uses Power Associated with his/her/their Position Appropriately

As we progress in our career, we sometimes forget our position gives us legitimate decision-making ability, budget, evaluative responsibility, the ability to assign or take-away resources, fire/

hire talent, or general credibility based on our credentials. Some of the most genuine and I think soft spoken physicians receive frequent feedback that they are seen as intimidating. Support staff, patients, and the general public will assign power to people with positions or credentials that they respect. Most leaders with power have dedicated 10,000 hours to mastering a skill set that others admire. Over time, experience will allow you to quickly assess, compress and make rapid decision-making. Our inner wisdom becomes refined with life experiences. Using your intuition wisely will help you be perceived as using your power associated with your role appropriately.

MINDSET CHALLENGE:

Listening to your self while listening to others takes discipline. Consistently remind yourself that, "Even if I do not know all the facts or understand the current challenges/barriers, I can make an imaginative leap or educated guess about a likely outcome, solution, or pattern. Even if it seems uncertain, I can test my ideas and ask others to provide both opposing and supporting facts and information."

Leaders who have strong intuitive awareness are those who can access deeper wisdom and rapidly synthesize information patterns and events to make decisions that add value to oneself and others. Intuition is the experience of having an idea or sense of something that can be a guide in moments of uncertainty or rapid change or can support decision-making when time for analysis is limited. Effective intuition balances rapid, accurate integration of both thoughts and feelings.

- Consider opportunities that allow for more reflection to develop greater self-knowledge about your emotional triggers and preconceptions. Faulty decisions can be made when you confuse an intuition with an emotional reaction that may be connected to some other event or personal issue.

- Allow yourself to take scheduled breaks from thought-intensive work so that you can relax and make a mood change. Very often, when people shift their focus away from work, the very issue they have been working to understand can emerge in a new thought or image.

- "Meditation" is gaining great interest in the business world because it is a form of mental focusing that allows leaders space for reflection, where they can confront emotional charges with compassion rather than judgment. As little as 9 minutes of quiet reflection a day, for as little as three weeks, is considered useful for becoming clearer and less emotionally reactive.

- "Mindset" is your way of responding to the world, according to your beliefs, assumptions, and attitudes. How open are you to the idea and value of intuition? How willing are you to engage in activities that may be unconventional but may rely more on intuitive responses?

- Differentiate between cultural and emotional biases and intuition. Being aware of one's biases and emotional triggers is a way of protecting against faulty decision-making that may seem intuitively right but may need further exploration.

People who have a natural proclivity for intuition display some or all of:

1. Can list the general concepts first
2. Are attracted to the new and untried
3. Emphasize the theoretical
4. Desire change

5. See problems as opportunities to innovate based on inspiration

6. Focus on the future possibilities of a situation

7. Want to know what could be

8. Value imagination

9. See the future costs and benefits

10. Desire information on how trends can predict future

11. Focus on outcomes

12. Focus on the meaning of what happened

13. Notice subtleties

14. Look at patterns

A gratitude journal or other form of journaling helps you tap into many of the dimensions of awareness including, self-awareness, emotional awareness, and intuition. On the more analytical side, practice thinking of new strategies your organization can take to be even more successful in the future. Strategic planning, focus and priority setting usually helps a team establish an intuitive climate.

Accurately Portrays Information

Our research has helped us define 10 different ways to accurately portray information. A truly balanced leader needs to employ all of the languages of influence and adapt according to the listener. Psychological safety is enhanced when a leader balances asserting with listening. A leader who is too assertive will appear aggressive and erode trust. A leader who listens but rarely asserts will appear passive—avoiding the toughest issues. Those Leaders who can synthesize other's perspectives into themes as they are sharing information will foster followership.

Mindset Challenge: How well do you organize your rational thoughts. Consistently remind yourself that you can more precisely use logic, facts, evidence, and other proof when communicating.

The Languages of Influence™[40] must be mastered as the second half of the leadership equation.

To grow both psychological safety bubbles and foster accountability you will need stakeholders in all directions to help you get an idea adopted. People tend to be comfortable with a repertoire of about 4 styles of influence; expand your repertoire to expand your leadership. To be influential you have to have a clear point of view and be willing to work with other people. People will want to support your ideas when they feel heard and understood. Some of the influence styles require more listening. Some of the influence styles require more assertion. Some of the influence styles focus on building relationships and connecting with people's values. Others rely on analytics and logic. Begin by defining success for yourself. Think about your career goals and where you get satisfaction from your work. Focus on areas that support your success and career satisfaction.

The psychology of influence is based on some simple human principles: consistency, reciprocation, social proof, authority, and liking.[41] Influence is personal—and interpersonal. That is, you can hone your skills to be more influential and choose to communicate with people who understand your intentions. People should know that they will have the opportunity to influence you as well. There are manipulative forms of influence and collaborative forms of influence—how you influence depends on you. The most powerful types of influence are not manipulative. Influence can be assertive without being aggressive. A good influence attempt will usually benefit the influencer and the influencee—and therefore be collaborative.

---

[40] Executive Core and Singer, Psychological Safety and the Languages of Influence.
[41] Cialdini, Robert B. Influence: The Psychology of Persuasion, 1993. http://cds.cern.ch/record/2010777.

People use ineffective tactics repeatedly to influence those around them. When you're trying to persuade someone, do you ever feel like you're beating your head against the wall? You probably are. After collecting data from more than 9,500 professionals about how well leaders influence others, we've found that leaders consistently use inappropriate or ineffective influence tactics. In their research, Yukl, Guinan, and Scottolano gathered descriptions of influence attempts from 215 people employed in various professional settings. Yukl and his team discovered, "In a surprising number of incidents the agent used pressure or legitimizing after encountering initial resistance when another tactic would have been more appropriate." In their research Yukl et al., found that consulting and appealing to values were seldom used for gaining support although these methods would have been highly effective.[42]

- Those who have a clear concept of their own values are less likely to be swayed by rational persuasion (Porter et al. studies this numerous times).

- Inspirational appeals create followership and are needed to communicate vision and strategy.

- Rational persuasion gets adoption of ideas at more senior levels—it's the currency of upward negotiations.

- Consultation, acquainting, and exchanging help achieve task commitment and are most effective. These top three work well at all levels.

- Inspirational appeals have been shown to be less effective when influencing upward in numerous universities and corporate studies.

---

[42] Yukl, Gary, and J. Bruce Tracey. "Consequences of Influence Tactics Used with Subordinates, Peers, and the Boss." Journal of Applied Psychology 77, no. 4 (August 1, 1992): 525–35. https://doi.org/10.1037/0021-9010.77.4.525.

- Consulting is used less upward but co-building solutions have been found to create long-term commitment. Some studies suggest that if you let a more senior stakeholder know that the project is well underway and their contributions are key to finishing the project, they will be more likely to help. If they also see that their early contributions helped the process along, they tend to be even more committed.

"The will to be totally rational is the will to be made out of glass and steel: and to use others as if they were glass and steel."

—Marge Piercy, Founder of the Movement
for a Democratic Society

You have the ability to influence people around you. You have natural talents and skills that contribute to that ability. You may or may not have a multimillion-dollar advertising budget to help you communicate, but you do have some very powerful personal abilities.

Think about the people who have communicated well and consistently portrayed information well. Chances are some of these people greatly influenced your life. They were probably unaware that they were influencing you as deeply as you now report. What did they do that was so influential? Why did their behavior impact you so greatly? Why don't more people impact you that way?

The reality is that most people have a small repertoire of influence skills they use over and over again. Do you try to logically persuade everyone you need to influence? Or do you try other ways to influence people—appealing to values or their friendship, building alliances of supporters, etc.? Sustaining psychological safety will require that you first understand your proclivity for communication. Which four styles do you use most? How would you master the ones you use less? Finally, how well do you listen for cues that signal the type of communication people want? Consider your organization's list of influences. There may a tendency for people in your organization to value some of these languages over others. In healthcare organizations, relationship building, asserting, and rational persuading are usually important. Physicians become used to asserting action to care for patients but true influence often happens informally through mutual respect and friendship among ecosystems of medical professionals. In highly regulated industries or the legal profession, legitiziming is likely to be valued. People appreciate the letter of the law and need to articulate how a request is consistent with the law's intent. Identify critical people in your life with whom you communicate. See if you can identify which three styles of communication they prefer. How could you get better at growing your psychological safety bubble by communicating with them in a way they can hear and appreciate?

10 Languages of Influence™

Rational Persuading

Using logic, facts, evidence and other proof to substantiate your request.

Cue: What's the rationale? Can you weigh the pros and cons?

Inspiring

Connecting your request to others' values or beliefs.

Cue: Why is this important? How will people be impacted? Our decision is guided by a number of important principles.

Consulting

Incorporating another's ideas into your request or co-building a solution with them

Cue: I have some thoughts about this. In my experience... I'd love to help. Interesting. Let's discuss this some more.

Acquainting/Socializing

Discovering commonalities with another, learning more about their point of view.

Cue: Tell me a bit about your background. It's a small world. What do you do outside of work?

Exchanging

Explicitly agreeing to share something or negotiate something.

Cue: What give and take do we have in this situation? Here's what I'm trying to achieve. I'd love to help but...

Personal Appeal

Asking a person for a favor or assistance simply on the strength of the relationship or history you have with the person.

Cue: At its best, the person will almost automatically grant a request just on the strength of the relationship as long as it's in their power and ethical.

Coalition

Some call this a type of leadership: building a group of supporters to show social proof that an idea or suggestion is worth adopting.

Cue: What does the rest of the team think? Who else supports this?

Legitimizing

Citing an outside authority or even your authority, a policy, or procedure when making a request.

Cue: What standards have been specified for this? Is there a policy? What does our leader think?

Asserting

Asking for what you want clearly.

Cue: What specifically do you need and by when?

Coaching

Guiding, teaching, or showing someone how to do something.

Cue: Can you show me how? I'd like to figure out how to achieve that. I've been stuck and looking for solutions.

– Executive Core Languages of Influence 360° assessment[tm]

Think about a normal day. What in your life depends on the cooperation of others? You depend on others for the quality of your medical care, food, shelter, clothing, social needs, getting ordinary tasks done at work, paychecks, roads, safety, and so on. Your ability to communicate in a psychologically safe way greatly impacts the quality of your life. You can't turn back when someone says no. Influence also involves knowing how people want to be asked. Influence also involves being open to change when your influence strategy isn't working. And most importantly, it means remaining open to influence. When you do something for someone, they later feel obligated to reciprocate. Random acts of kindness have been noted to cause infectious goodwill. More importantly they reinforce your mindset and resilience to build psychological safe bubbles wherever you go. Do three random acts of kindness today and tomorrow. Encourage everyone on your team to do the same. Then, talk about communication and psychological safety. Positive goodwill and benign intent without hope for reciprocity fuels the green bubble.

A technology leader commented,

> *"I recognize the importance of self-awareness and adjusting my approach based on the audience. I understand as a leader that I need to adjust how I influence and not always be in the driver's seat in a discussion to highlight my cognitive ability. I will recognize my stakeholders' communication and working styles to support the best output for our team. I want my team members to view me as adaptable and recognize my ability to adjust my contributions to meet the needs of the team."*

Communication and influence involve carefully listening to others and being open-minded—which sometimes leaves you vulnerable and open to their ideas. Although sometimes risky, this approach continually breeds excellence by fostering a collaborative environment. One of my favorite mantras is if first you don't succeed, try something different. Psychological safety bubble building may start with you and your mindset, but psychological safety across a project is a team sport. It sparks leadership across the team. Consider measuring everyone's ability to grow a psychologically safe bubble on your team. When the majority of the team maintains the skills associated with psychological safety, they spark leadership among others outside the team. Think of the last sports competition you watched. After the game, you can observe leadership sparking across competing teams by watching individual atheletes give authentic and heartfelt congratulations to athletes on the other team.

Chapter 4

How to Measure
Psychological Safety

"What gets measured gets done, what gets measured and fed back gets done well, what gets rewarded gets repeated."

— John E. Jones

In 2024, we studied trends in our global database of high potential leaders (N= 1,000) and found that the average high potential leader was still in the yellow zone for psychological safety. And an alarming number were clearly close to the 3.3 threshold for derailment because of their inability to build psychologically safe zones.[43] You will recall that when you measure psychological safety, you can correlate it to financial performance, employee engagement, customer retention, and employee retention. We measure psychological safety using our 360° assessment called Psychological Safety & the Languages of Influence™.

---

[43] Executive Core and Singer, *Psychological Safety and the Languages of Influence.* (Group Report 2023)

Psychological safety without accountability is not sustainable. The Languages of Influence™ are your pathway to ensuring both bubbles are strong.

Sensitivity to feelings is currently the Achilles heel for most leaders as the lowest rated competency. Many leaders struggle to find time to make a positive impact on peers. A leader's ability to help their colleagues come up with new ideas," is the lowest impact rating in our database during the time of writing this edition. More leaders are perceived to be out of balance by using too much asserting rather than listening. To build accountability and psychological safety in leaders, much can be done to grow one's rational communication, inspiring people to get excited about the future and show them how it aligns with what they value. Leaders need to get better at building coalitions of followers all working to a common goal.

Keeping the measure simple has been a critical aspect of measuring what really matters.

While self-assessments are useful, they are only as accurate as our self-awareness. It is advantageous to ensure that your immediate team gets feedback about the psychological safety others think they build. In most cases our intentions don't always match others' perceptions.

I have been studying predictors of leadership success most of my career. Leaders who are fast-tracking in their career are generally one standard deviation above the norm for a subset of factors that foster innovation, collaboration, psychologically safe working bubbles (upward with senior leaders/boards, laterally with peers, and also with direct reports).

We recommend that you measure your own ability to develop psychological safety and the other leadership skills that foster sustainability by taking the Psychological Safety and Languages of Influence™ online 360°.

- Based on 20 years of data collection taken from over 250,000 high potential leaders—40% outside of the U.S. more from private sector but also from public sector/national labs/and DOD contractors

- Based on 50 years of study of the psychological principles of influence

- This current version of the assessment was validated with C-suite and SVP high potential leaders in collaboration with our work with the University of Toronto—Rotman School of Management
   - Technical report summarizes high levels of validity

- Leaders benchmarked against over 1,000 successful senior leaders VP and above in large global organizations

You might be able to identify themes that are relevant and unique to your company. To holistically evaluate leadership that centers around psychological safety, I recommend that you consider five scales:

1. Basic psychological safety skills

2. Impact on the organization, team, and individuals

3. Balanced communication (listening and asserting)

4. Predictors of leadership success

5. Self-awareness

A person's flexibility in changing their style has been a stable predictor for success in our assessments. The most successful leaders tend to reinvent themselves over time. Education may also be a factor when influencing others. PhDs are perceived as more effective when rationally persuading, using logic even more frequently than those with lower levels of formal education, and PhDs tended to be perceived as having more reputation and knowledge power than others. People with an undergraduate degree only from a university tended to build stronger relationships than the other categories.

Beyond this, there were very few differences in influence appropriateness, frequency, or effectiveness. We have also studied the languages of influence across cultures in various countries. Interestingly, all translate well although how they are expressed varies. In summation, if first you don't succeed, try something different, educate others about your communication/influence preferences, be open to influence, and if you can't be sincere with an influence style, don't use it.

When evaluating how well people are developing bubbles of psychological safety, it's useful to do this with an intact team. You can review the results individually and collectively. It's also useful to see how well people build psychologically safe and accountability bubbles with colleagues more senior than them. Psychological safety and accountability bubbles that expand to stakeholders and VIP's who are more senior or powerful than you is a great way to collaborate when you have less power. Peers need psychological safety and accountability bubbles just as much as your team members and direct reports. Select respondents carefully when taking a 360° assessment.

Currently in our database, the good news is that adhering to high ethics is the highest rated item for high potential leaders. However, when we study the lowest rated items, interesting patterns emerge that suggest there is a growing call for high potential leadership to be better defined by one's ability to grow an umbrella of psychological safety. In general, we are seeing a greater call to leadership who can build coalitions of followers, prioritization, and inspiring people by describing a compelling vision for the future:

Consider the pivotal priorities (goals), people (select your respondents carefully), environment/situation surrounding these people, how self-aware and open are the people being evaluated, and is accountability present? Does everyone have clear roles, targets for change, and ways to measure their pivotal priorities over time?

When debriefing the assessment, we like to use the GREAT model. Ask people about their:

Goals

Respondents

Environment (You are Currently in)

Awareness level & Defenses

Targets for Change

Simply by seeing how a person rates themselves against other's ratings foster self-awareness.

"I am a more literate, self-aware leader. I now understand that an authentic, effective leader is one who continually engages in the lifelong commitment of developing himself or herself, while also bringing along and nurturing the development of others. In striving to become the best version of myself, I will make daily choices based on my personal values and the shared values of the organizations of which I am a part. My colleagues will not only see me making these

daily decisions, but more importantly, they will also see the sum of these decisions consistently made and compounded over time. I will routinely re-examine how I can be "a force for good." In the future, people will identify me as an authentic and valued leader and someone who they enjoy working with and can seek out for advice and perspective."

−Leader from a top 5 Consulting Firm
After Receiving feedback, coaching,
within the psychologically safety bubble

Even if it isn't practical to use our customized 360° that looks at the comprehensive factors behind building bubbles of psychological safety, at the minimum pulse your team using the psychological safety competencies we shared earlier in the book. When you do have good metrics, you can compare results alongside organizational pulse surveys, performance reviews, KPI achievement, and financial results. Using some data analytics like cluster analysis, you should be able to identify high potential talent. Feedback highlights that they have mastered leadership in a very comprehensive way so that the people around them are inspired to their best every day and achieve ambitious goals.

Stratus is a nationwide brand implementation company that makes lighted signs and brand remodels of spaces for some of the largest companies in the country. They are growing rapidly and are backed by private equity. While under pressure to grow sales, the company realized the leadership needed to grow along with an increase in valuation. Here's how they measured their leaders' psychological safety bubbles and applied the concepts in this book.

We were very concerned about talent loyalty and how attrition was impacting Stratus' performance. COVID was still a thing, which had a domino effect on supply chain and inflation, wage growth and the Great Resignation, [and] the dramatic shift to a hybrid work model. We sought outside expertise to consult us on talent management strategies."

Executive Core's engagement launch included an innovative executive team workshop designed to provide leadership insights, including a "Trip to Mars" exercise to help them identify key leadership attributes.

"Executive Core's sometimes uncomfortable 'Trip to Mars' meeting blew open the doors to the great work we've done this year to align business and talent goals. Our 'Trip to "Mars' exercise involved deciding who we would send to Mars to successfully and independently run our company there— without ongoing help from 'Earth Stratus HQ.'"

Executive Core helped Stratus realize that they needed to better understand, measure, and train key leadership attributes. We studied the business, developed assessments, and identified the attributes that drove performance in Stratus' highest performing divisions:

- Highest levels of psychological safety
- Lowest employee turnover
- Highest customer retention
- Higher employee pulse data

The very highest performing division excelled across the board. They enjoyed not only the highest psychological safety, but also performed highest in key performance metrics, had less than 7% regrettable loss, the happiest customers, and the highest profitability.

Executive Core utilized our data-driven approach to coach leaders and provide custom hybrid education for ongoing leader and team training. The approach with Stratus:

- Educates everyone about psychological safety
- Discloses how it will be measured cross leadership
- Measures individual and team performance—with professional debriefing & development plans
- Provides "Coach & Create" learning forums based on psychological safety
- Assesses and ranks all relevant people, and their financial performance
- Measures individual and team improvements over time
- Rewards high-performing leaders
- Provides for continuous improvement

All the work supports, measures, and extends Stratus' five "Values in Action," building behavioral competencies that enhance the Stratus learning culture.

–Tim Eippert,
CEO Stratus and Maureen Woodarski, SVP of HR

I once knew a leader who had high IQ and terrific analytical skills. When not working for a top five consulting firm, he spent a great deal of time in meditation at a Zen retreat in the West coast. Yet he had very little awareness of how his peers experienced his behavior as arrogant and detached. 360° feedback helped him spark leadership within himself and then it was contagious to others in his career. Gazing in the mirror doesn't create self-awareness—inner and outer dialogue and feedback is necessary. Self-awareness is the super-predictor of leaders who spark leadership in others.

Chapter 5

Coaching Others to Grow Bubbles of Psychological Safety

"It is not fair to ask of others what you are not willing to do yourself."

—*Eleanor Roosevelt, United Nations Diplomat, humanitarian, and first lady*

Now that the people around you know what psychological safety is, they have practiced it, been measured against it; now is the time to coach them on sustaining it. Over time, you should see organizational culture improve. First, you need to make sure you have solid performance mindsets in order to be a coach. Otherwise, your own bias and blind spots will interfere with success. Then make sure the people around you are ready and receptive to your coaching. If you haven't adapted your languages of influence well enough or balanced listening and asserting well enough with a person; you may not be the best candidate to coach them.

Coachability

To spark leadership in others, be coachable. Encourage coachability in others. But don't force coaching on those who don't want it or who aren't ready. Here is a simple method of identifying a person's coaching readiness.

COACHING READINESS QUIZ

As you prepare to complete your Awareness 20/20™, take this quiz. It will help you get into the right mindset to receive the feedback. You can also use this to evaluate others' coaching readiness as you develop and grow others.

COACHING READINESS Not ready at this time	1	2	3	4	5	COACHING READINESS Extremely ready
My Level of Trust in Coaching Nonexistent	1	2	3	4	5	High
My Openness Long history of not accepting feedback	1	2	3	4	5	Life long learner
Business Need No urgency	1	2	3	4	5	Clearly advantageous to the business
Belief (in coaching) Highly skeptical	1	2	3	4	5	Seeks out coaching
Adaptability Fixed mindset	1	2	3	4	5	Seeks to understand self and constantly evolve and change
Outlook Fears prevent openness to change	1	2	3	4	5	Excited about positive outcomes of change
Psychological State Highly stressed, burned-out, major life event	1	2	3	4	5	Healthy state (full capacity to work, love, play)

Anyone that averages a 3 or lower may not be receptive to coaching. After setting expectations that building a bubble of psychological safety is expected from all team members, you may have to choose an alternative approach. When you are clear that standards of psychological safety and accountability are necessary to be a part of the team, you may have to have performance discussions instead of coaching. In some cases, individuals who are borderline coachable will benefit from taking the coaching readiness assessment above. It may motivate them to open themselves up to new possibilities. If you are an experienced executive coach, you might introduce the concept of coachability and initiate a discussion early in the relationship about a person's coachability. At some moments in life, a person may be burned out, having challenges in their life, going through a divorce, grieving the loss of a loved one, suffering from mental wellness challenges, or battling addiction issues. In these cases, the person will need support beyond coaching.[44] [45] Being sensitive to these moments in life is part of growing your own bubble of psychological safety. Being creative with scheduling so that you can move projects forward when team members need to step out temporarily is a common challenge teams face. Having some cross-training among roles allows people to cover for one another and attend to life outside of work. It's also an opportunity to give someone a stretch assignment if a team member is temporarily off work. That likely means you'll be coaching more. Don't forget to remind the team that onboarding and psychological safety are team sports.

I crave moments to reflect and gain substative feedback in environments where I feel safe. I suspect you might, too. Most of us take too little time to reflect. My best friend of 45-years invited me to join her on a writing/meditation retreat in a refurbished monastery on an Umbrian mountain top. We left our young families behind with loved ones and went on to discover amazing vistas, morning yoga, silent breakfast, silent writing marathons, afternoon feedback sessions, alfresco vegetarian meals (and a few glasses of wine). This led to wonderful memories, reciprocal coaching, and profound feelings of safety, adventure, and accomplishment. We often joined one attendee in the evening

---

[44] Griggs, Korie. *Suffer Well: Poems for the Grieving. VK Press. 2022.* Korie Griggs wrote the dedication poem for this book and uses prose to explore the waves and complexity of individual and collective loss.

[45] It is not a bad idea to have some resources on hand for just such an occasion.

to sit quietly and watch the sunset. He radiated positivity and exuded warmth in broken English each time we greeted him. Later, we learned he was near the end of his life with a terminal diagnosis from cancer. Life is short. Savor it. Embrace it. He reminded me that even in your last days you can leave people better than you found them.

Coaching Needs Compass[46]

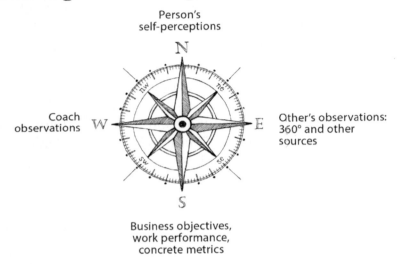

Person's self-perceptions

Coach observations

Other's observations: 360° and other sources

Business objectives, work performance, concrete metrics

Not everything is worth coaching. If you observe specific behaviors that are opposite of the psychological safety factors, coaching is likely helpful. Before coaching it is helpful to have your observations to share, understand how the person sees themselves, have good quantitative and qualitative data about how others perceive the person, and show a clear work performance that needs to change.

---

[46] Bacon, Terry, and Karen Spear. Adaptive Coaching: Client-Centered Approach to Performance Improvement. Interviews & research excerpts by Barbara Singer. Palo Alto, United States of America: Davies-Black Publishing, 2003.

Using this needs compass can you find clear and specific examples about how a person is and is not:

- Adhering to high ethics
- Being authentic
- Demonstrating willing to discuss tough issues
- Refraining from intellectual bullying
- Accurately portrays information
- Using power associated with his/her position appropriately
- Creating an enjoyable atmosphere
- Showing sensitivity to others' feelings

Do your homework. If you haven't gathered information using all four poles of the needs compass, spend more time reflecting, collecting others' insights, and observing. Again, a 360° evaluation is one of the most efficient ways to make sure you are focusing on areas that matter to your work group.

The GREAT Model

Also prepare to coach by formulating your questions. In a study I did early in my career, published in the Adaptive Coaching book, we discovered that most leaders preferred 60% non-directive coaching and 40% directive coaching.* People don't want to be told what to do. In a coaching conversation they hope to gain insights they would not have gotten on their own, new possibilities they hadn't considered before, and more holistic perspectives. The GREAT model may help you organize the conversation in a way that fosters these preferences. What are your GOALS? What is the status of your RELATIONSHIPS?. I can imagine that a few may be in under performance discussions with you that may detract from their feelings of psychological safety. Tell me more about the team and market ENVIRONMENT? I noticed you rated yourself much lower than how everyone else rated you. Are you AWARE that this may be a defense mechanism designed to motivate you to achieve under extra stress/fear of failure? What are your TARGETS FOR CHANGE as a result of our discussion? Just remember GREAT and you'll always have a coaching road map.

Goals

Relationships

Environment (You are Currently in)

Awareness level & Defenses

Targets for Change

You might find some ideas for focus by identifying when leaders are "below the line." See the appendix for more information.

When people are not creating the best psychological bubbles of safety themselves, you will have to enter into more challenging coaching discussions. Interestingly, you will need to calibrate how much assert versus how much you listen to help get individuals back above the line and able to promote their own psychological safety bubble for others. For people who are avoiding or not accurately portraying information, you are going to have to be more directive with your observations of their behavior. Be specific. What have you directly heard them say or seen them do? Be crisp in your observation without a lot of pre-qualifiers. "I noticed that you haven't talked more than 5 minutes in our last three team meetings. You looked at J. a long time when he was explaining why he hadn't been able to finish his part of the project and rolled your eyes at A." The effect seems to be that you're avoiding the need to collaborate with J. and speak up in team meetings about what your group needs." Pause. Suggestion: "Tell me what else is at play here? How can we develop an environment where everyone is on the same timeline and shared understanding of the deliverables? What have you tried? Avoiding the situation doesn't seem to be making it any better."

In one engagement I read over 250 performance reviews. It confirmed what I suspected—even organizations known for proactive feedback watch employees fail because they can't find a way to tell them something is wrong. As a coach it is important that you can appreciate people's effective performance 3 x the 1 x you give them feedback to improve. [47]

If a person is damaging the psychological safety bubble by being intellectually sniping, verbally micro-aggressive, or even physically aggressive, you might need to listen and show empathy before they are willing to collaborate with you in a psychologically safe bubble you build.

When you master coaching psychological safety, you should be able to do it with intact teams while everyone is all together. I like to build the agenda around the following formula and use all the techniques we have discussed in this book. It was clear through Michael Ensley's study of over 4,500 companies, attributes of team interactions predict financial performance[48]. And of all the

[47] Barbara Singer, "The Evolution of the Traditional 360 Feedback Process," ed. Lore International, Lore White Paper Series, 1927.

[48] Ensley, Michael D., and Keith M. Hmieleski. "A Comparative Study of New Venture Top Management Team Composition, Dynamics and Performance between University-Based and Independent Start-Ups." Research Policy 34, no. 7 (September 1, 2005): 1091–1105. https://doi.org/10.1016/j.respol.2005.05.008.

attributes, trust is foundational. Since then, we have connected our focused list of optimal team interactions to more innovation, better company culture, prevention of regrettable talent loss, and agility when market conditions change. Spend time to understand each team's unique set of objectives and unique challenges. Ascertain:

- Does the team have a close bond outside of the meeting room, and support each other personally? Can people observe the strength of social relationships among members?
- Does everyone on the team engage in problem solving, productive dialogue, and (when needed) intense debate?
- Does everyone on the team embrace and seek out the degree of challenge being offered by the leaders? Does the team refrain from complaining about nonessential matters?
- Are team members assisting other members with their needs and projects outside of their function? Do they go the extra mile to coordinate efforts between team members?
- Does each person take accountability for the quality of the team experience? Does the team share the responsibility for challenging the status quo, so that no one team member bears all the burden or becomes stereotyped as overly negative?
- How well does the team foster fun, humor, and improvisation to promote more creativity?
- How well does the team keep an optimistic picture of the future even when setbacks occur?

- Is there clear communication prior to a team meeting, so people can hit the ground running?
- Does everyone on the team contribute an equal amount?

I recently worked with a top team responsible for $1Billion in revenue. When I started the project, their roles and ownership of tasks were blurred. They often failed to keep the customer's needs in focus by trying to uphold old procedures. They experienced frequent conflict, frustration, and reported hurt feelings among several members. This team worked hard using the techniques in this book to establish great psychological safety, performance, and collaboration. After several months of team meetings, assessment, and coaching; they came together to celebrate everyone's accomplishments. I knew we had entered a new phase of performance when this highly educated and experienced group of people initiated a rousing icebreaker of rock, paper, and scissors. Losers became cheerleaders for those who won each round. Laughter and cheering was contagious. As they worked through laborious RFP and selling processes, they had fun. The revenue followed.

Strategic Conversations

Appreciate the past
State the current situation
Provide a vision for what the future can look like
Plot a path forward

We first taught this formula to executives at American Express as some of the newly promoted executives prepared for townhall meetings. Organize your key points to a group in this way and you cover many styles of influence and appeal to people with different operating styles.

As a coach growing bubbles of psychological safety in others, you have the chance to also work with teams and not just individuals. I like to call it coaching in plural. Teams who collectively generate strong psychological bubbles collaborate well with other teams. They are often seen as driving change and naturally build coalitions of support across your organization because members are pleasant and fun to work alongside. I like to hold each team member accountable to the elements of building a psychologically safe bubble. Team dynamics tend to test the bubble. Interactions are ripe for making observations that reinforce the effort it takes to generate a psychologically safe bubble. You can use the tools in this book to:

1. To facilitate team effectiveness one team at a time

2. Set team expectations and a charter for future work and interactions to speed decision-making and information sharing

3. Explore best practices among teams who outperform and commit to new ways of working to foster psychological safety and appreciation

When working with a team you have the chance to accomplish the following:

- Trust
- Alignment on shared vision and goals
- Clarity of roles
- Stakeholder management
- Communication practices
- Norms
- Meeting management

- Inclusion
- Psychological safety
- Style/personality assessments
- Conflict resolution
- Plan development and implementation

Remember that top performing teams have the following characteristics:

- Have psychological safety
- Roles, responsibilities, and prioritization are clear
- Have space to learn
- Team members refrain from complaining about nonessential matters
- People think strategically—they can take on the perspective 2 levels higher in the organization and 4 years in the future with multiple scenarios
- People have a dense web of interpersonal relationships and can get things done quickly through collaborative efforts
- Teams act as bridges and trusted advisors across the organization and with suppliers and partners
- Team members speak candidly and then support decisions publicly and privately
- Team members go the extra mile to assist other members with their needs and projects outside of their function
- Treat onboarding as a team support—avoiding sink or swim experiences
- Coach, grow each other, and have fun together!

Team Events to Grow Psychological Safety

Here is a formula you can use for getting ready to help a team while fostering a bigger bubble of psychological safety.

Prepare

- Announce the focus for the team development
- Send messages to the team about what to expect and introduce the facilitator/team executive coach

Gather Feedback

- Coach conducts phone interviews to collect feedback from team
- Coach reviews previous insights regarding the team

Review Results

- Debrief call with team leaders
- Summarize themes and development opportunities for the team
- Develop an agenda and approach; communicate this in advance to the team

Team Offsite

- Tailor topics as needed
- Facilitate trust building activities
- Share findings and themes that emerged during the interviews
- Introduce team's best practices and tools
- While discussing the year's initiatives, apply approaches to evolve the team's performance
- Facilitate discussions that clear the air and tap into each person's strengths

- Agree how the top team will focus, communicate, make decisions together, and support one another's success
- Observe progress and provide ongoing feedback

Using Executive Core's Performance Mindset cards (similar to the mindset challenges I gave you earlier in the book), you can challenge the team to test their assumptions and bias. It's helpful to have the team focus on the future instead of allowing people on the team to become emotionally hijacked (and hijacking the agenda) by overly rehashing past conflicts in a public setting. I recently worked with a team that was experiencing high levels of conflict between an engineering function and a legal function. It was clear in their offsite that they did not establish ground rules for maintaining psychological safety.

Months later the conflict was still festering. Ask people to rate their consistently most reliable mindset and the two mindsets that are difficult to maintain on very bad days. Then have the team discuss ways to promote adoption of the performance mindsets on any given day.

The Michigan Health & Hospital Association (MHA) Keystone Center embarked on a High Reliability journey with many of our Michigan Hospitals. There were large and small, rural, suburban, and urban, teaching and community, academic and critical access hospitals, with the required common denominator of an engaged top leader, committed to this High Reliability process.

The organizations that best developed the traits of a Highly Reliable Organization were those whose leaders were most visible, transparent and engaged. These leaders were connected with their leadership team and employees at all levels of their organization, every day, regardless of their responsibilities. Within these organizations a culture of trust ensued, and objective surveys demonstrated employees felt psychologically safe and believed that they could best provide the care to their patients and assist their loved ones.

–Gary Roth, DO and Chief Medical Officer for the Michigan Health and Hospital Association

I am confident that smart teams that establish true psychological safety, are held accountable to maintain it, and are equally accountable for getting results; can accomplish almost anything. Teams that have trouble maintaining psychological safety may demonstrate creativity to achieve incremental change. But teams that truly maintain psychological safety can be motivated to radical creativity. Who might you extend a bubble of psychological safety to and what would it mean to stretch your thinking? What new zones of psychological safety might you establish that could be transformative for your organization?

Chapter 6

Psychological Safety Fuels Diversity & Inclusion Work

During the Covid Pandemic lockdown, after George Floyd was murdered, I was privy to the discussion among several prominent Fortune 100 executive leadership teams and their CEO's about how to respond. The country and their employees were shocked and grieving. I am encouraged that there was consensus that something needed to be said, but if you recall during that time many CEOs had letters "leak" to the press about how they felt about the situation. Their reluctance to fully own their words and their company's position, publicly discouraged me. Psychological safety came into clearer focus for me during this time. It also inspired me to write this letter as a CEO regarding my own response. I want to thank Dr. Stacy Jackson whom I've heard lecture over 20 times on standing tall for your values and being willing to sacrifice for them. His inspiration and teachings were woven into my response.

I'm sending this letter to my associates, my clients, and my network. I simply could not stand by without issuing a statement to call us together for action against injustice occurring in the United States. I ask each of you to take time to reflect. Our world is challenged by Covid-19, an uncertain economy, and now we find other issues to be illuminated. The time for talking about change is long overdue. Today is the day to do something small to live the change. And recommit each day to continue doing something small to live that change. It starts with what is in your head and your heart. Challenge your beliefs that no longer serve the higher good of society. Then act peacefully and decisively to change something that is unjust. Your true intentions are judged by your actions; not your words. Finally, have some impact on the systems you operate within in your own organization. It is only then that we can celebrate change in a culture that needs to improve health, education, fairness for all, and economic stability for all people regardless of color, sexual orientation, gender preference, religion, and economic status.

Injustice is here. We are deeply bound to one another throughout our communities and states. We talk about, "We are all in this together." The truth is that many people are left out. We are all in this together when we look alike, share similar bank accounts, have achieved similar levels of education, have similar access to technology and education, have safe homes, and are judged on our performance not our outward characteristics. We think as long as we protect the status quo, our families, cities, and towns will be safe. The irony is that we are at a pivotal point in history where without change for the good of all, we forget we are caught in the web of interconnectedness. Elinor Claire "Lin" Ostrom remains one of the first of only two women to win the Nobel Prize in Economics for her ideas on having economic governance to manage our global, shared, and interconnected resources. People have a right for psychological safety. When they feel safe, included and a sense of belonging; people can go to work and do their very best. This is a great time to be a bubble maker.

During this same time I was approached by Ramona Hood, the CEO of FedEx Custom Critical Care to join 28 days of intense conversation about race and leadership. Ramona is one of the few black female CEO's represented among the nation's top companies. We were joined by a group of extraordinary "Divas" that became my friends and taught me much about myself and psychological safety. They also became my personal advisory board on unconscious bias and inclusion. They challenged me to make a difference. I would be remiss if I did not name each of them.

Ramona Hood, CEO FedEx Custom Care
Dr. Rachel Talton, CEO, speaker, and expert on all things diversity equity and inclusion
Nichole Marshal Chief Diversity Officer of Bath and Body Works (Now CDO for Pinterest)
Carmen McGhee, Chief Operating Officer at the National Association of Investment Companies (NAIC)
Linda L. Hsu, Chief Operating Officer and Firm Administrator at Chico & Nunes, P.C.
Christine Lobas, Chief Executive Officer of Studiothink

Assuming you look us up on LinkedIn, you will see that Christine and I were the only leaders who were not black or brown. When we could finally be together at Dr. Rachel's home, I remember one afternoon full of laughter when someone blurted out about me that she didn't realize, "white people had so many problems." I don't think I fully understood my position of privilege although I had been representing women in leadership most of my career. It was a humbling and loving journey, full of grace and empathy. Ramona shared her journey to CEO and the challenges it presented as she formed her top team. Nichole shared her challenges finding resources to make DEI a priority across her company despite the CEO advocating for her role strongly. Carmen and I often discussed how little private equity funding was being allocated to women and black and brown entrepreneurs. Linda was our conscience and questioned our assumptions. Christine shared her own stories and put a marketing lens on how we could better communicate our passions. Linda challenged us to consider the Asian American Pacific Islander community and the model immigrant myth. This was particularly poignant for me as my youngest son is half Chinese American and has experienced racism during the China bashing days of the Covid-19 pandemic.

Me, I was and at the time of writing this book am still involved in the Diversity Equity and Inclusion Task Force sponsored by the Executive MBA Council Board. At that time our joke on the EMBA board was that I had become the poster child for gender parity in graduate business education. My friends in higher education and my new business leader friends were stretching my beliefs, assumptions, and understanding of the world. During one meeting I can recall Nichole Marshall who was SVP of Diversity at a well-known brand admitted she was exhausted and did not want to talk about diversity, equity, and inclusion anymore. The rest of us were silent. Those brave black female leaders were tired. Nichole and our band of sisters challenged each other to take action and do something that would result in measurable change. I am proud to say that the Executive MBA Council published a guideline on DEI best practices for business schools. I am proud that I wove DEI into the Executive MBA curriculum at Notre Dame and began fireside chats with our students about the topics. The divas would drop in from time-to-time by Zoom. Another friend and colleague of mine from the Executive MBA Council diversity task force wrote this poem to describe her experience being the "only" in the room and persevering when psychological safety has been in question for her.

When You See Me, Who Do You See?

I am told, time and time again, that the world does not see color. So, when you see me, who do you see?

You say that Black and White are just crayon colors, keys on a piano, a song written by Paul McCartney and Stevie Wonder . . .or is it?

As a little girl, or boy with much melanin grows, their lives become more difficult. Is it the speech, the diction, the hairstyle, the clothing? But society is color blind? So, do you see me or am I invisible? I can't be invisible if you point out my attributes that are displeasing to you, your school, and your organization.

When you see me, who do you see?

Rosa Parks fought so I can get a seat in the front of the bus but how do I get a seat at the board table? My BS, M.B.A, PhD is more than anyone else in this organization, but I'm constantly shown that the empty seat cannot be filled by someone with my melanin.

The white women got cut by the glass shattering their ceiling and I cannot seem to penetrate this concrete one. Dr. Ladson-Billings, Kimberlé Crenshaw, bell hooks . . .they not only coined the terms, even gave some an acronym and no one is listening. Intersectionality, Critical Race Theory (CRT) and Black Feminist Epistemology (BFE).

To where do we go and who do we fight to obtain that thing called "justice"? But, if I raise my voice or even "fight" for my own freedom, much less my brother and sisters, I get labeled the "angry black woman."

When you see me, who do you see?

You have told me that my time is coming. But when will that be? My brother's and sister's are being shackled, killed unnecessarily for walking in their own skin. We are "not enough" to attain positions despite having the highest levels of education. My God! Yes, my God . . . He is who I seek because man continues to fail me, systemic racism prevails, inequity in school lives, and neither my laboring, nor letters after my last name cannot get me that seat at the table!

When you see me, let me tell you who you need to see . . .

A black woman who is not defined by her color, but owns it. A beautiful black woman who is humble, speaks with intelligence, strength and wisdom. A black woman who observes you with discernment, who has achieved and is continuing to achieve every ounce of success to remain competitive in your very own landscape. Be not afraid, but understand that I no longer want a seat at your table. As my Father had many mansions, I have created my own table with many seats.

So, now I ask, when you see me, who do you see?

By: Dr. Dina C. Skeffrey

I trust that you will find your passion to change and influence and be thus inspired.

But in Elvis' words, "a little less talking and a little more action" was what was needed. I am most proud of my collaboration with Dr. Leon Jackson, former Chancellor at St. Joe's College in Indianapolis and a former Notre Dame student of mine. We worked together with a team of amazing leaders and colleges to start the Diversity in Leadership Program. Diversity in Leadership has become his passion.

With just over 1,500 candidates who have applied to our program, selected black and brown leaders and female leaders participate in a seven-month jumpstart program that prepares them for graduate education. Many of the universities involved provide intensive learning weekends hosted by their best faculty for the delegates. During the program, delegates complete the Psychological Safety and Languages of Influence™ 360° and participate in executive coaching. We use all the principles in this book to create a safe bubble for the delegates to learn and grow. Our goal for the program was to accelerate leaders into top of the house roles by completing graduate business education, growing their leadership self-awareness, building their executive mindset, and even becoming certified in psychological safety tools. What is also interesting about these cohorts is that their stakeholders rate them among the highest for building bubbles of psychological safety compared to other teams and groups we survey.

We vet delegates by identifying leaders that fit the criteria for executive MBA programs. Delegates are selected by those who have major contributions to their communities and who identify as members of an ethnic minority group or women. Each must:

- Have earned a bachelor's degree
- Have 7+ years of work experience

- Have 3+ years of supervisory experience
- Are positioned for rapid advancement in their careers.

This criteria satisfies the requirement for admission for most Executive MBA programs so has also been of value to schools who want to recruit more diverse candidates. We pre-vet and prepare them for the universities. The program has generated over $3 million in scholarship money, diverse enrollment in business schools (among those that participated) increased by 70%, their program's enrollment in general increased by 20%, applicant GPA's averaged 3.5 or higher, and we've seen 17 people promoted to the C-suite in their organizations. 18 new businesses have been started and one delegate received a $50 Million grant for their nonprofit work while in the program. 84% of the delegates were promoted during the course of the program with 37% receiving significant salary increases. The University of Notre Dame, Purdue, Butler, the Kelley School of Business at Indiana University, Xavier, The Ohio State University, University of Cincinnati, Case Western Reserve, MIT, the London Business School, Marian University, Howard University, the Ross School of Business at University of Michigan, University of Toledo, Miami University, Kent State University, and the Kellogg Business School at Northwestern have all been involved in offering learning modules and sponsoring the program. What made the difference? Bubbles of psychological safety grew among the group, among the schools, and in the community.

It has been my honor to personally coach and work with each cohort to date. Their stories, struggles, and resilience have been transformative for me. I think I could write another book simply about my own experiences in this program. For now, I'll simply challenge you to first establish a zone of psychological safety, and then talk less and act more. You will find your own passion projects. I am confident you will discover the rewards of pushing outside of your comfort zone.

As leaders we can use our own bubbles of psychological safety as platforms to grow the good in business and in our communities. We may not always agree with each others' perspectives or assumptions, but listening deepens our appreciation for one another. I like to think as our mind opens to new possibilities, our hearts become more empathetic. It was this kind of thinking that drove me to articulate my firm's values more than 14 years ago. I hope the values of my firm will live on long after I am gone and that the leaders who follow them grow vast bubbles of psychological safety as they travel the world. I can espouse these values but the real challenge is to find ways to live them each and every day. I guess that's why I'm writing this book. I've talked a lot about "setting the learning free™" over the years. Now we need to set psychological safety free as part of that mission of encouraging people to share openly what they learn.

Values

Generosity

We don't hold back. We give freely of our time, thought, experience and knowledge to the extent that our clients need it. We don't hold things in reserve to extend an assignment or secure the next contract. We share what we have learned very openly with our clients, and enable them to better share what they have learned from us very openly with others around them.

Graceful

We deliver the greatest impact for clients with the most efficient level of energy investment on the client's part, and maximize the seamlessness, elegance and calmness in every interaction and suggestion we make. Many of the issues we work on with clients carry high levels of stress and emotion; we minimize this everywhere possible to maximize objectivity.

Encouraging

We avoid negativity wherever possible. All our client interactions are marked by a focus on positive action rather than reaction, and we provide all our clients with a supportive framework and partnership to support them as they drive forward in their careers and professions.

Candid

One of the biggest challenges for leaders within organizations is that the information they are presented with by subordinates and peers is often modified to reflect the needs & preferences of the provider, and driven by an (often invisible) agenda. We make the daily choice to be the one person in a client's world whose feedback, shared observations and advice are not colored by a need to 'stay friends', and we guarantee candor even if the feedback isn't necessarily delightful at the time. We value truth over niceness if we have to choose between the two; we let our clients down and break our covenant with them if we are anything other than completely candid.

Loving

We make the daily choice to love our clients – both organizations and the individuals. This has a specific meaning and value for us: in a business driven by recommendations and word-of-mouth, success for our clients is success for us. Our clients' objectives are our objectives; we do ask permission to help clients shape and refine their own understanding of their objectives, but once that is done we partner with them and dedicate ourselves to achieving their goals.

There is an old adage that 'CEO' really stands for 'Clients, Employees, and Owners—in that order.' We practice this when we work with our own clients, helping them to focus on stakeholder needs in that order, and we practice that same prioritization ourselves. Building psychological safety goes beyond positively impacting direct reports. Psychological safety bubbles can be manufactured for people much more senior than you, peers, suppliers, customers, the community, our families, and our friends. In the end, psychological safety provides a backdrop for influence and positive change everywhere. When sustained, it should lead to happier employees, happier teams, and environments that foster mental wellness where people can show up and do their best. And psychological safety will make us better thinkers because we invite new perspectives to the table and keep them there by making them welcome. Best wishes on your own personal journey and I hope that I have encouraged you to leave people and places better than you found them. I hope your bubble will be remembered long after you have left the room.

About The Author

Barbara Singer is the recipient of the Global 2013 Executive Coaching Thought Leader of Distinction award from the Association of Corporate Executive Coaches, a 2023 Inductee in the Coaching Hall of Fame, Faculty of the year award at Notre Dame for the graduating Executive MBA class in 2017, and the 2018 Flourish Female Entrepreneur of the Year. Barbara is the founder, president, and CEO of Executive Core and leads a group of global professionals whose mission is to more quickly innovate professional development globally for corporations and business schools alike. In the last 30 years, Barbara has worked with thousands of high-potentials leaders around the globe at critical turning points in their careers. She is an expert on future trends in learning and has been researching predictors of executive success for nearly two decades. She has been the corporate liaison on the board of the International Executive MBA council three times made up of business schools from around the world. She has helped lead the diversity board for the council.

Barbara has conducted research on global influence, and executive coaching for nearly three decades, and has worked with three of the five largest international executive search firms responsible for placing a large majority of C-suite executives. She still thinks it's amazing that she gets paid for what she loves to do. She has five, yes, five children and a wonderful husband, Bob.

Acknowledgements

To my friends and colleagues who contributed thought thoughts and words to this topic

My Notre Dame Students

The Health Care Leadership Program Delegates

The Diversity in Leadership Candidates for Graduate School

The Diversity Diva's

My Manbassadors

Jeremy Jones

Sara Campbell

My international cadre of consultants

Chris of Fidello

Najeeb Ahmad

The Association of Corporate Executive Coaches

Ellen Flint, Graphic Designer

Foxie of Mars

Alex former McCormick

Leon Jackson, PhD

Executive Core clients who teach me to keep my mind open every day to see new possibilities.

Bibliography

"A Guide to Responding to Microaggressions – Women in Engineering," n.d. https://wie.engineering.illinois.edu/a-guide-to-responding-to-microaggressions.

Bacon, Terry, and Karen Spear. Adaptive Coaching: Client-Centered Approach to Performance Improvement. Interview by Barbara Singer. Palo Alto, United States of America: Davies-Black Publishing, 2003.

Black, Michele C., Kathleen C. Basile, Matthew J. Breiding, Sharon G. Smith, Mikel L. Walters, Melissa T. Merrick, Jieru Chen, and Mark Stevens. "National Intimate Partner and Sexual Violence Survey." 2010 Summary Report, January 1, 2011. http://hdl.handle.net/20.500.11990/250.

Bruch, Heike, and Sumantra Ghoshal. "Beware the Busy Manager." PubMed 80, no. 2 (February 1, 2002): 62–69, 128. https://pubmed.ncbi.nlm.nih.gov/11894679.

Cialdini, Robert B. Influence: The Psychology of Persuasion, 1993. http://cds.cern.ch/record/2010777.

Clance, Pauline R, and Suzanne A. Imes. "The Impostor Phenomenon in High Achieving Women: Dynamics and Therapeutic Intervention." Psychotherapy: Theory, Research

& Practice 15, no. 3 (n.d.): 241–47. https://doi.org/10.1037/h008600.

Cline, Ernest. Ready Player One, 2011. https://bibliotheques.vyvs.fr/recherche/viewnotice/id/35815/clef/READYPLAYERONE-SPIELBERGS-WARNERHOMEVIDEO-2018-4/retour_avis/14.

Cooper, Cynthia. Extraordinary Circumstances: The Journey of a Corporate Whistleblower, 2008. http://digilib.umpalopo.ac.id:8080/jspui/bitstream/123456789/407/1/0470124296__Extraordinary%20Circumstances%20The%20Journey%20of%20a%20Corporate%20Whistleblower.pdf.

Ensley, Michael D., and Keith M. Hmieleski. "A Comparative Study of New Venture Top Management Team Composition, Dynamics and Performance between University-Based and Independent Start-Ups." Research Policy 34, no. 7 (September 1, 2005): 1091–1105. https://doi.org/10.1016/j.respol.2005.05.008.

Executive Core, Singer Barbara, and Dorothy Siminovitch. "Awareness2020." Executivecore.Com. Executive Core, 2018. Accessed November 21, 2023. https://executivecore.com.

Executive Core, Singer Barbara, and Dorothy Siminovitch. "Awareness2020." Executivecore.Com. Executive Core, 2018. Accessed November 21, 2023. https://executivecore.com.

Executive Core, and Barbara Singer. Psychological Safety and the Languages of Influence. 360° assessment. 2.0. Executive Core, 2023. https://executivecore.com.

"Five Fifty: Is It Safe? – Desktop," n.d. https://ceros.mckinsey.com/is-it-safe-desktop/p/1.

Gallup, and Ryan Wendell. "Employee Engagement Strategies: Fixing the World's $8.8 Trillion Problem." Workplace, September

11, 2023. https://www.gallup.com/workplace/393497/world-trillion-workplace-problem.aspx.

Global Talent Trends: Data-Driven Insights Into the Changing World of Work. "Global Talent Trends: Data-Driven Insights into the Changing World of Work," n.d. https://business.linkedin.com/talent-solutions/global-talent-trends/archival/global-talent-trends-october-2022.

John, Doerr. Measure What Matters. New York, United States of America: Portfolio/Penguin, 2018.

Kouzes, Jim and Association of Corporate Executive Coaches. "Everyday People, Extraordinary Leadership." Slide show. https://acec-conference.org/award-recipients, n.d.

Kruger, Justin, and David Dunning. "Unskilled and Unaware of It: How Difficulties in Recognizing One's Own Incompetence Lead to Inflated Self-Assessments." Journal of Personality and Social Psychology 77, no. 6 (January 1, 1999): 1121–34. https://doi.org/10.1037/0022-3514.77.6.1121.

LinkedIn and LinkedIn Talent Solutions. "2022 Global Talent Trends." The Great Reshuffle, 2022. https://business.linkedin.com/content/dam/me/business/en-us/talent-solutions-lodestone/body/pdf/global_talent_trends_2022.pdf.

Luqmani, Adam R., Matthew Leach, and Da Jesson. "Factors behind Sustainable Business Innovation: The Case of a Global Carpet Manufacturing Company." Environmental Innovation and Societal Transitions 24 (September 1, 2017): 94–105. https://doi.org/10.1016/j.eist.2016.10.007.

McKinsey Health Institute. "Moving the Needle on Burnout: What Does the Data Say?" McKinsey & Company, 2022.

https://www.mckinsey.com/mhi/our-insights/moving-the-needle-on-burnout.

Melikian, Ana. "The PIE Method." Blubrry Podcasting, September 1, 2023. Accessed October 10, 2023. https://anamelikian.com/the_pie_method/.

Metaverse Standards Forum. "Code of Conduct - Metaverse Standards Forum," April 17, 2023. https://metaverse-standards.org/diversity-and-inclusion/code-of-conduct.

On Disney+. "Rogue Trip," n.d. https://ondisneyplus.disney.com/show/rogue-trip.

Singer, Barbara. "Preventing Executives at Risk of Derailment." Lore International White Paper Series., 1993.

Singer, Barbara. "The Evolution of the Traditional 360 Feedback Process." Edited by Lore International. Lore White Paper Series, 1927.

Singer, Barbara and Iowa Hospital Association. "The Promise of Psychological Safety for Better Workforce Engagement And Performance." Workforce Engagement. Https://My.Ihaonline. Org/Events/Calendar-of-Events. Des Moines, United States of America, n.d. https://my.ihaonline.org/Events/Calendar-of-Events.

Singer, Barbara and Lore International. Personal Influence. 2nd ed. Awareworks, 2004.

Singer, Sara J., Shoutzu Lin, Alyson Falwell, David M. Gaba, and Laurence C. Baker. "Relationship of Safety Climate and Safety Performance in Hospitals." Health Services Research 44, no. 2p1 (March 12, 2009): 399–421. https://doi.org/10.1111/j.1475-6773.2008.00918.x.

Sull, Donald, Charles Sull, and Ben Zweig. "Toxic Culture Is Driving the Great Resignation." MITSloan Management Review, January 11, 2022. https://sloanreview.mit.edu/article/toxic-culture-is-driving-the-great-resignation/.

Torrance, E. Paul. "Torrance Tests of Creative Thinking." Data set. PsycTESTS Dataset, July 9, 2012. https://doi.org/10.1037/t05532-000.

Van Dyne, Linn, Karen A. Jehn, and Ann Cummings. "Differential Effects of Strain on Two Forms of Work Performance: Individual Employee Sales and Creativity." Journal of Organizational Behavior, December 12, 2001.

Walters, Mikel L., Jieru Chen, and Matthew J. Breiding. "The National Intimate Partner and Sexual Violence Survey: 2010 Findings on Victimization by Sexual Orientation." Data set. PsycEXTRA Dataset, January 1, 2013. https://doi.org/10.1037/e541272013-001.

Washington, Ella. "Recognizing and Responding to Microaggressions at Work." Diversity and Inclusion, May 10, 2022.

Yukl, Gary, and J. Bruce Tracey. "Consequences of Influence Tactics Used with Subordinates, Peers, and the Boss." Journal of Applied Psychology 77, no. 4 (August 1, 1992): 525–35. https://doi.org/10.1037/0021-9010.77.4.525.

APPENDIX

	TEAM ROLES	STAKEHOLDERING	TEAM INTERACTIONS	PRIORITIZATION	STRATEGIC PARTNERS/ ALLIANCES	CULTURE
ABOVE THE LINE	Clear on each team member's role, its requirements. Team leadership, behavior, focus, priorities, style, and accountability adapt in sync with market changes. You have a well-prepared hand-off strategy for the next team who continues the work.	Team members are well coordinated in how they foster relationships and communicate with key stakeholders. The team acts as trusted advisors to customers (internal/external outside partners—leading to a solid working relationship and alignment that empowers effective implementation of strategy.	As your team grows, morphs, changes; team members openly appreciate each others' contributions, coach skill sets, and coach and inspire each other to grow. The team leader can make tough resource re-direction without unnecessary hesitation.	The team knows their 1-3 strategic priorities and aligns people around them. Strategic priorities are road mapped with metrics established over time so work can be anticipated and scheduled well. The organization and teams are willing to sacrifice time and budget to ensure these strategic priorities pay off.	Identify strategic partners, resources, and other entities that forward the team's mission in the hearts and minds of the customers (internal/external). These relationships often lead to mutually beneficial outcomes like revenue, brand awareness, more customers served, and innovation.	People make solid decisions together quickly, you see high employee engagement metrics, and evidence that targets/timelines are being hit. Regrettable talent loss is low (less than 15%) and people move fluidly to stretch assignments, have fun, form close friendships at work, and remain positive under pressure.
BELOW THE LINE	Fail to realize the full scope of ownership and each team member's role, fail to take a mindset tow levels higher, fail to focus on key metrics monitored by a dashboard, becomes distracted by tasks that are not big bets/high payoff, do not move the project forward. Difficulty delegating or finding time to grow support from other teams.	Achieve only subject matter expert status with stakeholders, supervising leader, customers (internal/external) outside partners and project teams. Fails to be fully invited to the table on strategic decision making. May report information that is of partial consideration.	Team works independently, protects locus of control, and does not feel as if they belong. People focus on the majority of their time on the discrete day-to-day tasks and don't see the bigger vision. Team members are reactive and often negative. Team members become very siloed as they work–even more pronounced if you have dispersed locations/ hybrid employees.	Team remains distracted up to 80% on busy work like returning emails and activities not connected to the strategic priorities. Fire fighting, protecting turf, slow reaction time to changing market trends, uncoordinated decision making, waste and rework, silo mentality, and lack of trust. Teams fail to push back when strategic priorities will be impacted.	Majority of partners achieve surface level success only. People fail to acknowledge the importance, some lose interest, walk away and sunk cost occur. Teams chase partnerships regardless of strategic focus or positive impact on mission. Partner agreements and relationships suffer and may disintegrate. People blame outside forces.	Decisions are made by very few people and tend to be top/down. You may begin to see mistakes happen because decision makers fail to communicate/inform/ identify risks/or ask for help. Team members ask to be reassigned or even leave the organization. There is little time to celebrate team successes. Signs of burnout and negativity are apparent.

Psychological Safety Scale

Check your selection

	SOMETIMES	MOSTLY	ALWAYS
Adheres to ethics	○	○	○
Is authentic	○	○	○
Is willing to discuss tough issues	○	○	○
Refrains from intellectual bullying	○	○	○
Accurately portrays information	○	○	○
Uses power associated with his/her position appropriately	○	○	○
Creates an enjoyable atmosphere when working with others	○	○	○
Is sensitive to others' feelings	○	○	○

LOW   AVERAGE   HIGH

Based on the majority of your responses above, which zone might you place yourself?
Place an "X" at the appropriate spot on the gauge.

Printed in Great Britain
by Amazon

45644598R00091